A HISTORY OF
CHRISTIANITY IN ENGLAND

HUTCHINSON'S UNIVERSITY LIBRARY

CHRISTIAN RELIGION

EDITOR:

REV. PROFESSOR E. O. JAMES

M.A., D.D., D.LITT., PH.D., F.S.A.

*Professor of the History and Philosophy of Religion
in the University of London*

A HISTORY OF
CHRISTIANITY IN ENGLAND

by

E. O. JAMES,

M.A., D.D., D.LITT., PH.D., F,S.A.

PROFESSOR OF THE HISTORY AND PHILOSOPHY OF
RELIGION IN THE UNIVERSITY OF LONDON AND
FELLOW OF UNIVERSITY COLLEGE. EXAMINING
CHAPLAIN TO THE BISHOP OF WAKEFIELD

HUTCHINSON'S UNIVERSITY LIBRARY
11 Stratford Place, London, W.1

New York   Melbourne   Sydney   Cape Town

THIS VOLUME IS NUMBER 24 IN
HUTCHINSON'S UNIVERSITY LIBRARY

Printed in Great Britain by
William Brendon and Son, Ltd.
The Mayflower Press (late of Plymouth)
at Bushey Mill Lane
Watford, Herts.

CONTENTS

PREFACE

In no country in Europe is the religious situation quite so complex as in Great Britain where Church and State have grown up together from the beginning of the Christian era as the two most important factors in the development of the national life and character of our island civilization, carrying on a tradition grounded in the pre-Christian foundations of British culture. It is only possible, therefore, to understand the position when it is reviewed in the light of the historical circumstances which have been responsible for giving English Christianity its peculiar shape and form. Regarded superficially and as a contemporary phenomenon, English religion is an enigma. The National Church often appears to be either an irrational political compromise, or a *via media* which is neither completely Catholic, properly Protestant, nor consistently Liberal, except to those who hail it with delight and admiration as Christendom in microcosm, providing the pattern and prototype of a reunited all-embracing œcumenical Church, making possible as a real synthesis that which is of permanent value in all the uniting traditions.

In striking contrast to this comprehensive Anglican Communion, stands firm and erect the Roman Catholic edifice with its clearly defined doctrine and regulated faith and worship, but while no other section of English religion calls forth quite the same whole-hearted loyalty and enthusiastic devotion from its adherents, somehow for the majority of Englishmen it appears as a foreign institution which, like a townsman in a village, does not exactly "belong." On the Protestant side, there are the numerous non-episcopal communities, some of which are now grouped together under the general title of free churches, but their multiplicity is the occasion of considerable bewilderment to the uninitiated, and gives support to the widespread belief that Christianity in England is a city of confusion. So for not a few the situation resembles a jig-saw puzzle, and until the many pieces are put together as a historic construction it is impossible to understand the significance of the several parts and their relation to the whole design.

As Dr. Norman Sykes has said, the Church historian is concerned "with nothing other or less than Christ's holy catholic church, that is the whole congregation of Christian people dispersed throughout the whole world; and dispersed also through nearly twenty centuries of history, yet with a vital consciousness of the unity and continuity of its tradition." In this volume, therefore, an attempt is made to give a picture of Christianity in England in its widest aspects as a national growth first within the corporate life of the one great centralized organization, and later as a mutilated body with ever-widening divergences—doctrinal and administrative—among its component or independent parts. The story, however, happily does not end here. To-day, it would seem, the sectarian tendency is on the wane, and, notwithstanding the internal subdivisions, varying traditions and divided allegiances that have characterized English Christianity for the last 400 years, a new conception of a Christian fellowship is becoming visualized, extending into almost every nation and making possible a new and more constructive approach to many of the old controversies.

Since the primary purpose of this book is to give the general reader and the student beginning the serious study of the subject a kaleidoscopic view of the religious situation in England in the hope that thereby he may be led to make a more detailed study of the field for himself, a bibliography has been appended to each chapter as a guide to further inquiry. So far as the Church of England is concerned the best general history is that edited by Stephen and Hunt in nine volumes (published by Macmillans between 1901 and 1910), where the story is told with a fullness and accuracy that leaves nothing to be desired. Gee and Hardy have collected in a convenient form the *Documents Illustrative of English Church History* (1896), which should be consulted, while the eight volumes entitled *History of Religion in England*, by J. Stoughton, are a mine of information about the course of events, particularly in relation to Nonconformity, from the days of the Long Parliament to the middle of the nineteenth century. *A History of the Church* from the Roman Catholic standpoint, by Philip Hughes (Sheed & Ward, 1934–47) is in process of publication, the first three volumes of which, now in circulation, cover the period from Apostolic times to those of Luther. For the modern period, in addition to the works mentioned at the end of Chapters VII and VIII, biographies of outstanding religious leaders in England should be consulted. A *History of the Church of Ireland* from the beginning to the present day has been compiled under the editorship of W. A. Phillips (Oxford University Press, 1933) in three volumes, and Dr. A. R. MacEwen had reached 1560 in his *History of the Church in Scotland* (Hodders, 1913, 1918) before his death. Dr. G. D. Henderson has dealt with *The Religious Life in Seventeenth-Century Scotland* (Cambridge, 1937) and Dr. J. R. Fleming with the period from 1875 to 1929 in his *The Church in Scotland* (T. & T. Clark, 1933).

In the absence of documentation it has not been possible to indicate the precise sources of information to which I have had recourse in the preparation of the manuscript, but all the books that have been consulted are, I hope, included in the lists, as well as other important works bearing on the matters under review. Especially am I grateful to my friend and former colleague, the Rev. J. C. Dickinson, F.S.A., Fellow of Emmanuel College, Cambridge, for his help and advice and the many valuable suggestions he has made, particularly in the section that deals with his own period. To my wife I am indebted for her assistance with the marking of the proofs.

E. O. JAMES.

King's College,
    London, W.C.2

CHAPTER I

THE BEGINNINGS OF
THE CHURCH IN BRITAIN

WHEN St. Paul was establishing Christian communities in
the cities of Asia Minor and Greece, and finally in Rome, the
British Isles were in process of becoming an integral part of the
Roman Empire, which extended from the Euphrates to the
North Sea and from North Africa to the Danube and the Rhine.
Long before the arrival of Julius Cæsar on the beaches of Kent
near Deal, on 25th August, in the year 55 B.C., Britain, however,
had been in very intimate contact with the Continent and
had been the home of an advanced culture. Therefore,
so far from the Roman legions encountering hordes of wild
and savage "ancient Britons" with bodies painted with woad
and armed with primitive weapons, they endeavoured to gain
a foothold in a country that for more than 2,000 years had been
virtually part of the European continent with which it was in
line in its cultural equipment.

PRE-ROMAN BRITAIN

Since about 2,500 B.C., when the first invaders spread over the
chalk and limestone hills of Kent, Sussex and Wessex, and their
extensions in East Anglia and Yorkshire, introducing a simple
agricultural economy based on the cultivation of corn and the
rearing of sheep and cattle, waves of Continental people from
the earliest centres of civilization in the Middle East made
their way to Britain from Brittany, Portugal and Spain. Another
stream came from Central Europe along the Rhine to the Low
Countries and Northern France and thence to East Anglia and
the adjacent region, bringing with them the culture they had
acquired in their original homes. Intermarrying with the

11

native primitive population of the island, they collectively produced a civilization which was almost indistinguishable from that of the rest of Europe, except for certain characteristics which are peculiarly "British." Continental penetration, in fact, never succeeded in absorbing the indigenous culture, which to a remarkable degree revealed a combination of persistency and receptiveness. The final product was neither wholly Continental nor merely insular. Moreover, having enriched what it had acquired, it made its own independent contribution to Western civilization; exporting its wares and later its institutions and ideas, as well as importing what it required, or what was foisted upon it by invaders. This feature of British culture, deeply laid in the pre-Roman history of the islands, throws a good deal of light on the peculiar nature and characteristics of the Church in England as these emerged in later ages.

GLASTONBURY LAKE-VILLAGE AND ITS LEGEND

In the years immediately preceding the arrival of Julius Cæsar more and more refugees were driven to seek shelter in the camps and on the hill-tops of Britain, and in the lake-villages at Meare and Glastonbury in Somerset, as the Roman conquests on the mainland increased. A ridge of solid ground connected Glastonbury with a spur of the Mendips along which ran the main upland system of trackways leading to Wessex and Sussex. The Cornish tin mines were within easy reach of the adjacent coasts, as were Brittany and the Loire basin. Through the Bristol Channel only twelve miles away it is not improbable that immigrants from Brittany played a part in the foundation of this accessible and easily protected settlement, the influence and prosperity of which survived into the Christian era, when this part of Somerset was included by the Romans in their Belgic province.

As an important centre of commercial activity in close contact with both the Continent and the camps and hill-forts on the adjacent uplands of Britain, Glastonbury was well adapted for the development and diffusion of new religious ideas and customs. It is significant, therefore, that this ancient lake-village should have become the traditional cradleland of

British Christianity. Around it gathered a legend and a cultus in which the heroes of ancient folk-tales, such as King Arthur, Merlin and Percival, found their place in a Grail Romance associated with Avalon, the mysterious magic Isle of the Blest of Celtic mythology identified with Glastonbury and its famous Tor. These native traditions in due course were perhaps exploited by the monks of the great Benedictine abbey erected at the reputed burial place of King Arthur (i.e., Glastonbury equated with Avalon) as an offset to the parallel Grail romance connected with the relic of the Holy Blood of Christ current at the rival monastic house at Fescamp in France. In this way may have arisen the story related by William of Malmesbury between about 1129 and 1139, in which it is affirmed that in the year A.D. 63, at the instigation of St. Philip, Joseph of Arimathea with eleven companions arrived in Britain from Gaul and were given an island surrounded by woods and marshes, called by the inhabitants Ynys-Vitrin, and traditionally associated with Avalon and Glastonbury. There they built a church of timber and wattles at the foot of the tor in honour of the Blessed Virgin Mary. A century later this structure was discovered by two missionaries who were sent to Britain by Pope Eleutherius, and repaired by them to be used as a hermitage in memory of the original apostolic founders. The community, in fact, is alleged to have continued to occupy the site until the arrival of St. Patrick from Ireland in 433, who became the abbot and died at Glastonbury.

Another version of the story, which occurs in an ancient manuscript found in the Vatican and quoted by Baronius in *Ecclesiastical Annals*, brings Joseph of Arimathea with Lazarus, Mary Magdalene and Martha, in a mysterious boat from Palestine, like that which, in the Compostela legend, was said to have conveyed the body of St. James from Joppa to Padron, in Galicia in north-west Spain and made Santiago the most important centre of pilgrimage in medieval Europe. The company are said to have landed at Marseilles and proceeded through France to Britain, following doubtless the familiar overland trade route to the north-west as an alternative to that used by the Phœnicians via Portugal and Scillies to the tin region, as in the case of the Malmesbury tradition.

"The Three Perpetual Choirs"

The significance of these twelfth-century stories lies in the fact that they single out Glastonbury from all the great monastic churches of the period for the incident recorded. As we have seen, on archæological grounds there is good reason to surmise that this important lake settlement would be a very likely spot for Christianity to reach Britain from the Continent as a result of culture contact with the Middle East. Moreover, tradition also tells us that from time immemorial the worship of God was carried out unceasingly day and night before the coming of St. Augustine at the "Three Perpetual Choirs" situated at Glastonbury, Llantwit Major, in Glamorganshire, and at Amesbury, in Wiltshire. Now each of these three places happens to have been a very important centre in pre-Roman Britain, exactly where it might be expected that traders would congregate on their arrival in the island and disseminate new ideas and beliefs.

Glastonbury certainly fulfils these conditions, and Llantwit Major, or Cærworgan, as it was then called, was a similar site. The name Cærworgan suggests that it was originally one of the *Caers*, a title indicating a camp, fort or city, and this is supported by the fact that below the Norman church a Romano-British building has been found, together with ancient British encampments, dolmens and barrows. Furthermore, a network of trackways connect it with other extensive earthworks in the neighbourhood known to have been employed in the manufacture and trading of bronze and iron implements in pre-Roman times. There are also traces of the entrance to an ancient harbour which doubtless was the scene of numerous arrivals and departures from and to the Continent. The presence of coins of Claudius, Nero, Vespasian, Domitian, Trajan and Carausius at Llantwit, and in the neighbouring district, shows that the region was in contact with the mainland of Europe, and these connections were continued into the Christian era since St. Illtyd, the first abbot of the great monastic foundation of Llantwit Major (who has given his name to the place, i.e., Llanilltyd), was a Breton who is said to have been given sanctuary at this spot on the Glamorganshire coast and facilities for building a church and a stone wall above a fosse. Before he took up his abode there, according to one tradition he had joined the Court of King Arthur, and after he was converted to Christianity by St. Cadoc he collected round him such devoted disciples as Gildas, Samson and St. David. There are also references to Llanilltyd, or Llantwit, being an island which was united with the mainland by his miraculous intervention. Thus, in legend as well as in historical association, Llantwit Major and Glastonbury have much in common as ancient centres of the Church in Britain.

Similarly, Amesbury, the third of the "perpetual choirs," was situated in the heart of one of the most important regions in pre-Roman Britain, which since the erection of Stonehenge at the beginning of the Bronze Age, some 2,000 years before the commencement of our era, had been a hive of religious and secular activity with many comings and goings from and to the Continent. The famous stone circle on Salisbury Plain, less than two miles from Amesbury, in the first instance was the work of an early metal-using people, commonly known as the Beaker Folk (because of their use of a distinctive drinking cup). These people during the opening centuries of the second millennium B.C. settled on the chalk downs of Wessex, having come mainly from Holland and the Rhineland with contingents in all probability from Brittany. In addition to their continental contacts they and their successors had commercial intercourse with Ireland by way of Wales, and with the west of England, to obtain the valuable Cornish ores. During the whole of the Bronze Age and the succeeding Celtic Iron Age, in the third and second centuries B.C., the prosperous farming lands of Wessex continued to attract relays of invaders from Brittany and to have trade relations in all directions, extending from the Eastern Mediterranean, Spain, Central Europe and Denmark to Ireland. Stonehenge was rebuilt in its present magnificence, some of the sacred stones having been brought from as far distant as the Presely Mountains, in Pembrokeshire. When Druidism flourished in the first century B.C. this mysterious and greatly distorted Celtic priesthood which came to Britain from Gaul, may have used the ancient sanctuary for its rites, and so perhaps arose the popular error that the prehistoric monument was of Druid origin. In any case, at the time of the Roman invasion Amesbury was in the centre of a district which for 2,000 years had been a strategic point in the development of English civilization and religious practice. Furthermore, like Glastonbury and Llantwit Major, it was in close touch with continental influences and their cults, for Stonehenge was essentially a temple, as was Avebury, twenty miles away.

THE COMING OF CHRISTIANITY TO BRITAIN

It is, therefore, a locality in which it would be natural to expect an infiltration of a faith that was making its way westwards from the Middle East as part of a stream of culture following long established trade routes extending from the Mediterranean to Britain.

Thus, taking the evidence collectively, the ancient tradition of the "Three Perpetual Choirs" may be based on a historical fact, namely that Christianity was first introduced into England from Europe by traders, merchants, adventurers, invaders, and possibly persecuted converts seeking a refuge in the island, who established Christian communities in places like Glastonbury, Llantwit Major and Amesbury, where from time immemorial new cultural traits, religious ideas and forms of worship had become incorporated in British civilization. With the Romanization of the country soldiers and civilians who had embraced the faith also doubtless contributed their quota to the process.

It is only in a few isolated towns, however, that Christianity has left any tangible evidence of its presence in Roman Britain. A small rectangular building with aisles and a porch found at Silchester in Hampshire, dated in the fourth century, is thought to represent the remains of a very ancient church, as is an oblong structure with apse and narthex at Cærwent, in Monmouthshire. According to the Venerable Bede (673–735) "while the Romans were yet in the land" at Verulamium a church was erected of "admirable workmanship and worthy of the martyrdom" of St. Alban, that somewhat nebulous saint who has given his name to the Hertfordshire city in which he is alleged to have been the first Christian in Britain to lay down his life for the faith. At Canterbury, Christchurch is mentioned as having been in existence when St. Augustine arrived in Kent in 597, together with the church dedicated to St. Martin which the king, Ethelbert, is said to have given to his Christian bride, Bertha, at their marriage.

That the Romans continued to worship in their customary pagan manner in the towns they built and inhabited is clear from the altars, statues, inscriptions, representations of gods on coins and the remains of temples (including possibly subterranean mithræ, or temples of the Oriental mystery divinity Mithras) belonging to this period. The worship of the Græco-Egyptian goddess, Isis, in a temple in London is attested by an inscription, and the veneration of the Roman emperor Commodus as Hercules, and of cults of Mother-goddesses, are revealed by coins, statuettes and votive figures. The prevalence of paganism is also reflected in the widespread practice of cremation, and when inhumation became more common, the construction of the graves and the objects in them, follow along the lines of pre-Christian burials in the Mediterranean countries. Christianity, therefore, made very little impression on Roman Britain though from the third century it grew in strength until at length it became the best organized authority in the country.[1]

CELTIC CHRISTIANITY

Outside the Roman province Druidical and other Celtic rites were performed apparently in association with ancient stone monuments like Stonehenge and Avebury, and as Christianity gradually penetrated into this region it was doubtless at the local sanctuaries that Christian services were held until in course of time in all probability simple buildings were erected in wood and wattle and daub to serve as churches and oratories. But being made of perishable materials they have left behind no traces of their existence. Bede mentions a church of stone called *candida casa* at Whithorn, in Galloway,

---

[1]The Early Christian Father Tertullian about A.D. 206 affirms that "in districts inaccessible to the Romans people called Britanni had become subject to Christ," while in the previous century a rhetorical remark of Justin Martyr to the effect that every country known to the Romans contained those who professed the faith might be supposed to include their province in Britain.

B

erected in 397 "after a fashion unfamiliar to the Britons." This was the work of Ninian, a Scot who had been trained and consecrated in Rome, and who employed masons from Tours, in France, the home of St. Martin, to erect both this church and the monastery he founded there on the model of the continental religious house set up by St. Martin at Marmoutier in Gaul.

Although this monastic centre does not seem to have been a great success until it was refounded in the sixth century, there must have been a fairly vigorous Christian community in Galloway in the fourth century if, as is alleged, St. Patrick, the apostle of the Irish, was born and bred in the district about 372. In Ireland some progress had been made in the establishment of the faith, partly through intercourse with Britain, but also by direct contact with Gaul and the Mediterranean. Thus, the celebrated antagonist of St. Augustine of Hippo, Pelagius, was a Celtic monk whose heretical teaching had a profound influence in the country, and perhaps for this reason it was felt necessary to send a mission to restore the position. After an abortive attempt on the part of Palladius in 432, Patrick, a son of the sister of St. Martin, who had been trained at Lérins and Tours, landed and began his great work. Heterodoxy may not have been very deeply rooted but the struggle with paganism was long and bitter. So successful, however, was Patrick that not only did he lay the foundations which have stood the test of time, but he gave to Celtic Christianity as a whole fresh vigour and a new lease of life. Thus, from the fifth century the Church of the North-west was essentially the Church of Ireland and the adjacent British coastal region, linked with Brittany and the Loire by its Celtic affinities of culture, race, language, and monastic organization.

THE ANGLO-SAXON INVASION

When the Romans gradually abandoned Britain in the fourth and fifth centuries, the part of the country they had occupied slowly returned to prehistoric conditions. The towns became increasingly insecure, the hill-forts were refortified, and even Hadrian's Wall could not be garrisoned. From the numismatic evidence it seems the wall was abandoned in 383, and since no Roman coins have been found in the country at all later than 411, the official evacuation must have been complete by that date. Therefore, from then onwards the way was open for a fresh influx of invaders from the Continent—an opportunity seized by pagan Saxons, Jutes and Angles coming from the Low Countries and Saxony, between the Weser and the mouth of the Elbe—who in the succeeding centuries made themselves masters of the river valleys of eastern Britain and the adjacent district. It is possible some Saxon settlers took up their abode in the abandoned towns, but for the most part it was in the largely unoccupied territory that they established themselves and developed their superior methods of ploughing and cultivation. On the uplands of Cornwall, Wales and Strathclyde the Romano-British population survived, while Wessex, the Upper Thames Valley and the country round the Wash, and the intervening region along the Icknield Way, were Saxon, with a disputed region north and south of the middle Thames.

Thus, within a century of the Roman evacuation the Teutonic invaders had succeeded in establishing themselves in the eastern counties between Berwick-on-Tweed and Wessex, where apparently the great earthwork known as Wansdyke extending right across Wiltshire from the neighbourhood of Andover, in Hampshire, to Portishead, in Somerset, was constructed to protect the south-west of England as a Celtic stronghold. This represents a British tribal boundary behind which the Celtic Church developed its own traditions unmolested by the disturbing influences in the turbulent Teutonic part of the country in the east. The Roman type of diocesan organization was abandoned in favour of a monastic jurisdiction on the plan which had grown up in Ireland, where the Romans had never penetrated. This system probably prevailed there from the beginning, and after the Roman withdrawal from England it became the normal method in the Celtic world in the sixth century. From Wales, Devon and Cornwall it was introduced into Brittany, so that ecclesiastically as well as linguistically the west of Britain was again linked with the French Armorican peninsula (appropriately known as Brittany) as an independent cultural area.

CELTIC MONASTICISM AND ITS ISOLATION

For 300 years Dumnonia (i.e., Devon and Cornwall) maintained its integrity, while Wales and Ireland were never conquered by the Anglo-Saxon invaders. During this period of isolation Celtic Christianity took a firm root in the west, and in Cornwall alone it has been estimated that ninety-eight out of the 254 parishes now in existence are the descendants of the original monastic foundations. These monasteries were simple buildings arranged rather like the earlier Iron Age or Bronze Age settlements with a surrounding rampart enclosing a little church and a cluster of wooden huts or cells, occupied by each of the monks. In due course a library often was added as books accumulated, and eventually sometimes a school was built when teachers like St. Samson and St. Illtyd arose in an order. At first monastic life was as austere as the construction of the religious houses was primitive, the daily routine consisting of devotional exercises, study, the copying of manuscripts and heavy work on the land. With the accumulation of wealth, however, especially in Wales, the inevitable process of deterioration set in, and then even the rule of celibacy was not strictly observed.

Separated from the rest of Christendom, and confined within the very limited area that comprised the Celtic world in the sixth century, it is not surprising if the Church was out of touch with the mainstream of western Christian thought and practice. In developing its own tradition it had not unnaturally departed from Roman usages which had become established on the Continent. Thus, in such matters as the date of the observance of the Easter festival it followed the computation which had been in force before the old calendar had been superseded over the greater part of Europe by one based on more accurate calculations. Similarly, in the administration of the sacrament of baptism it had not adopted the customs upon which the Roman theologians had laid much stress, and it cut the tonsure of the clergy after a fashion that had become obsolete in the rest of Western Christendom.

These variations in custom, unlike the teaching of Pelagius, or that of the continental Reformers in the sixteenth century, were devoid of any doctrinal significance, but trivial as they may appear to be to us, they constituted a breach between British Christianity and the Latin tradition as it prevailed under the Roman jurisdiction. Consequently, when St. Augustine landed in Kent in 597 to begin the reconversion of the eastern part of the island, dominated by the English pagan invaders, he regarded the ways and methods of Celtic monasticism in the western and northern divisions of the kingdom as relics of barbarism and ignorance, and a challenge to the unity of the Church and its organization under the Papacy. When the situation was referred to the Pope, Gregory, for decision, Augustine was told to select and sedulously impart to his converts in Britain whatever he had been able to collect from local churches that was excellent, "for things," he said, "are not to be loved for the sake of places, but places for the sake of good things."

Furnished with this wise counsel the newly consecrated "Archbishop of the English nation" met the British bishops and reduced his demands to the three outstanding matters in dispute; namely, (1) the adoption of the Roman method of calculating the date of Easter; (2) conformity to the continental baptismal rite, and (3) that they and their flock should join with him in a united effort in the evangelization of the Saxons. Reasonable and desirable as these requests were, since their adoption would make for the consolidation of the Church as a whole, Augustine failed to take the measure of the men with whom he had to deal. Celtic Christianity, looked at from the standpoint of Roman organization, appeared as isolated, undisciplined and even barbaric, but it was full of vigour and extremely suspicious of anything that savoured of arrogance on the part of the newcomer. Moreover, it has to be remembered that it too had its continental contacts, its own powerful centres of learning and piety, notably in Ireland, its saints and its missionary enterprises which extended to the very gates of Italy. Therefore, in fact it was not as isolated as the Roman missionaries supposed. Consequently, it was not to be expected that it would change its time-honoured customs merely at the bidding of a very recently consecrated missionary bishop who, without any reference to them, had established himself in a remote corner of south-eastern England.

The Celtic and the Roman Traditions

The situation was further complicated by the fact that Irish and Scottish missionaries with whom the British bishops were in alliance were actively engaged at this time in founding monastic centres of sacred learning all over Western Europe, at such places as Anegray, Luxeuil, and Fontaines, in Burgundy, and subsequently at Bobbio on the other side of the Alps in the Ligurian Apennines, and at St. Gall in Switzerland, where they adhered to their own ecclesiastical peculiarities in total disregard of the Papacy, the Frankish Church, or the local episcopate. These lawless methods were not to be commended as they virtually produced a church within a church, but they were symptomatic of the Celtic temperament of the age, and explain the deadlock that ensued as a result of the Augustinian demands in England. They also show that the archbishop on his arrival at Canterbury was not wholly unwarranted in his endeavours to establish uniformity in practice and jurisdiction in the island of his adoption, though his efforts, not perhaps very wisely directed, ended in a lamentable schism which only increased the isolation and decentralization of the British Church. Furthermore, as Bede has revealed, the quarrel created a bitter antagonism on the part of the indigenous Celtic Christians towards those Saxons and Angles who during the succeeding period became obedient to the faith in eastern England. Thus, the country became divided into two diametrically opposed groups of professing Christians, the one looking to Canterbury as its centre, the other to Iona in the north-west.

Before the arrival of St. Augustine, a great monastery had been founded at Iona in 563 by St. Columba, which became the most powerful centre of Celtic Christianity and the home of a vigorous missionary enterprise. From it Aidan set forth in 635 to evangelize the Kingdom of Northumbria, and in conjunction with its devout king, Oswald, who himself had been educated there, reconstructed the Church in his domain, which had been forsaken by its first bishop, Paulinus. Together Aidan and Oswald laboured for the conversion of the rude Northumbrians, laying foundations on which others might build in less troubled times when the perpetual conflict with the adjoining Kingdom of Mercia came to an end in 651 with the defeat of Penda, the last pagan ruler in England until the Danish invasion.

THE CONVERSION OF ENGLAND

Meanwhile St. Augustine's work in Kent had not met with as much success as might have been expected from the good start made when the king, Ethelbert, and his thegns accepted the faith. The Saxons in south-east Britain had little real interest in the mission from Rome, and without being actively hostile they steadfastly refused to adopt Christianity except in isolated centres such as London, Canterbury, and Rochester. In these places bishoprics were established and in the seven years he occupied the Primatial See Augustine succeeded in laying the foundations in Kent which proved to be strong enough to withstand the strain placed upon them by the pagan reaction which set in after his death in 604. London, on the other hand, had to be abandoned and its bishop, Mellitus, having built a church there in honour of St. Paul, fled to Gaul with Justus, the first Bishop of Rochester. After remaining in exile for a year, they returned, but little progress was made in the evangelization of the country until the tide turned with the conversion of Edwin by Paulinus, the Bishop of Northumbria, and his deacon, James.

It was, however, the missionary enterprise of Iona that was responsible for the establishment of Christianity in the north and midlands. In the south and west only in Wessex, East Anglia and Kent was the Church of the Roman tradition able to make any headway, and in a sense it may be true to say that Aidan, the Celtic Bishop of Lindisfarne, rather than St. Augustine, the Primate of Canterbury, was virtually "the apostle of the English." But in fact there were two jurisdictions in the country, the Celtic Church holding sway in the barbaric north and midlands; the Augustine papal community prevailing in the more progressive south and west. But there was no unity; even the evangelists who came from the Continent—Felix from Burgundy to East Anglia, and Birinus from North Italy to Wessex—came independently, without seeking the consent of the successors of St. Augustine, while those in the north (Aidan, Chad, etc.) were not in communion with the rest. In the first half of the seventh century the British section was in the ascendance, but it rapidly lost ground owing to the lack of any properly unified territorial episcopal government in its monastic system. The bishops were merely missionary monks who went forth from their monasteries to evangelize, confirm, ordain and consecrate others to carry on the work regardless of all boundaries, to say nothing of Catholic order. In theory they were subordinate to the Abbot of Iona, but in practice they were laws unto themselves.

To the acuter minds of the younger men it soon became apparent that the Celtic tradition needed a radical reformation to rescue it from its insular isolation and to bring it into line with papal practice. The pioneer of this movement was a novice of Lindisfarne named Wilfrid, who had made a pilgrimage to Rome and thus become aware of the backwardness and stagnation of his native church by comparison with the vigorous and progressive ecclesiastical life of the Continent. In Rome he learnt about the vexed question of the date of Easter and had the monastic rule of St. Benedict explained to him. After spending some time in Lyons, he returned to England with the avowed purpose of carrying into effect the reforms on which he had set his heart and which to him seemed to be absolutely vital if the Church of the north-west was to survive at all. This involved, however, bringing British Christianity under the direct jurisdiction of the Papacy.

THE COUNCIL OF WHITBY

Installed as Abbot of Ripon, Wilfrid precipitated a crisis which led to the assembling of a Synod at Whitby in 663 to settle the matters in dispute. The Celtic side was represented by the Abbot and Bishop of Lindisfarne, Colman and his Scotic clerks, the Bishop of the East Saxons, Cedd, and the Abbess of Whitby. The advocates of the Roman position headed by Wilfrid included James the deacon and former companion of Paulinus, the son of Oswy, the King of Northumbria, the Queen's chaplain and two members of the Frankish Church. Oswy himself presided and Colman opened the case for the Celtic observance of Easter, basing his claim on a tradition supposed to have been derived from St. John the Apostle. To this quite fictitious argument Wilfrid promptly replied by claiming for his view the authority of the Blessed Apostle St. Peter on whom Our Lord had built His Church, and to whom He had given the keys of the Kingdom of Heaven. Added to this divine sanction, he contended that the Roman custom was observed throughout Christendom, "wheresoever the Church of Christ is spread abroad, save only among these and their accomplices in obstinacy, who foolishly, in these two remote islands of the ocean, and only in part even of them, strive to oppose all the rest of the world."

Thus, the argument was rested on the rival claims of the two traditions and the superior authority of the universal practice of the Continent over that of the isolated tradition of the British Isles. It was not difficult for Wilfrid to dismiss the alleged support of St. John for the Celtic Easter, and this left Colman only with the authority of St. Columba of Iona to pit against that of St. Peter. The king, as chairman, clinched the argument in favour of Wilfrid by asking the Bishop of Lindisfarne at this juncture "Did Christ really say 'Thou art Peter, and upon this rock will I build my Church, and the gates of hell shall not prevail against it, and I will give unto thee the keys of the Kingdom of Heaven?'" To this Colman was forced to assent and to agree that no comparable words were spoken to Columba. It then only remained for Oswy to declare, "for my part I shall obey the rulings of that doorkeeper of yours, lest haply when I come to the doors of the Kingdom of Heaven there shall be none to open them, he being my adversary who is proved to have the keys."

The case stated in these terms gave an easy victory for the Roman party, but although the theological arguments on both sides were puerile, the real issue was clear from the start. The choice lay between insular isolation and the wider influences and traditions of Western Europe. If the Celtic claimants had triumphed a considerable part of British Christianity would have been cut off from the mainstream of continental civilization and left to stagnate in its seclusion as a backwater. The victory of Wilfrid, therefore, marks an important turning point in English history, comparable in its effects to the invasion of the so-called Beaker Folk 2,000 years earlier, or to the Reformation 1,000 years later, when the position was reversed. But by their decision at Whitby the northerners not only abandoned their ancient customs, but they also put themselves under the Primatial See of Canterbury, as well as under the jurisdiction of the Pope. As Wilfrid was shortly to discover, for the next seventy years York was merely a bishopric which could be dealt with by the Primate like any other see, divided and subdivided as he wished, regardless of the views of the diocesan. Moreover, henceforth the scales were heavily weighted on the continental side, and while the island never ceased to endeavour to restore the balance, the odds against it were too great, until at length a fresh start had to be made to establish a new insular tradition on a very different basis and with only very limited success.

So far as the Celtic Church was concerned it received a mortal wound as a separate entity at the Synod of Whitby from which it never recovered, though it lingered on in a maimed condition in some of the monastic centres in Northumbria and at Iona, until some twenty years later the ninth Abbot, Adamnan, adopted the Roman usages and so opened the way for his successor, Egbert, an aged Irish monk, to establish the continental practice in the stronghold of north-west Christianity. In 716, for the first time in its history, Easter was celebrated at Iona on the same day as that on which it was observed in the rest of Western Christendom, thereby bringing the long drawn-out struggle to an end nearly a century before the great Celtic monastery was destroyed by the Norsemen in 802. The few monks who survived returned to Ireland with the relics of their founder, while in England the three streams of Christian faith and practice that had converged on the island, Celtic, Gallic and Roman, had become a single river carrying throughout the country the new cultural influences emerging in European civilization under the centralized control of the Church.

BIBLIOGRAPHY

Allcroft, A. H., *The Circle and the Cross*. London, 1920.
Bede, *Ecclesiastical History of the English People*. Ed. A. M. Sellor.

London, 1912. See also, *Bede: His Life, Times and Writings*. Ed. A. Hamilton Thompson. Oxford, 1935, for full bibliography.

Bulleid, A. and St. George Gray, H., *The Glastonbury Lake-Village*. 2 vols. London and Edinburgh, 1911–17. For a shorter account of the settlement see A. Bulleid, *The Lake Villages of Somerset* in "Somerset Folk Series." No. 16, 1924.

Childe, V. G., *Prehistoric Communities of the British Isles*. London, 1940.

Collingwood, R. G., *Roman Britain*. Oxford, 1933.

Collingwood, R. G. and Myres, J. N. L., *Roman Britain and the English Settlement*. Oxford, 1936.

Dearnley, M., "Roman Traditionalist Influence among the Anglo-Saxons," in *English Historical Review*. LVIII, 1943, pp. 129ff.

Duke, J. A., *The Columban Church*. Oxford, 1932.

Fox, C., *The Personality of Britain: Its Influence on Inhabitant and Invader in Prehistoric and Early Historic Times*. 3rd Ed. Cardiff, 1938.

Hawkes, C. F. C., *The Prehistoric Foundations of Europe*. London, 1940, with Kendrick, T. D., *Archæology in England and Wales*, 1914–31. London, 1932.

Hawkes, J. and C. F. C., *Prehistoric Britain*. London, 1948.

Messner, J. L. G., *The Celtic Church in England*. London, 1929.

Peers, C. R., "The Earliest Christian Churches in England," in *Antiquity*. March, 1929, pp. 65–76.

Plummer, A., *The Churches in Britain Before A.D.* 1000. Vol. I. London, 1911.

Sheldon, G., *The Transition from Roman Britain to Christian England*. London, 1932.

Stevens, F. *Stonehenge: To-day and Yesterday*. (Official Guide) Latest Ed. 1938.

Wheeler, R. E. M., *Prehistoric and Roman Wales*. Oxford, 1925.

Williams, H., *Christianity in Early Britain*. Oxford, 1912.

CHAPTER II

THE CONSOLIDATION AND UNIFICATION OF THE ENGLISH CHURCH

IF the immediate result of the Synod of Whitby was the vindication of the Roman tradition and of papal authority in the interests of unity, order and progress against stagnation and isolation, it was by no means an unconditional surrender to the superior continental powers. Civilization in the British Isles, as we have seen, for 2,000 years had been built up through a reciprocal process of absorption and renewal giving rise to new ideas and higher cultural achievements which in their turn were passed on to others. In this way an independent culture had developed which was essentially British and at the same time European, in the wider sense of being an integral part of the continental stream, so that it is possible to describe it by generalized names such as "Beaker" or "Megalithic," or by compound terms such as "Romano-British."

THE TWO TRADITIONS IN THE NATIONAL CHURCH

This process was repeated in the seventh and eighth centuries of our era when an English National Church began to take shape which owed its organization, discipline and practice to Western Christendom with its centre at Rome, but at the same time retained some of the most valuable ideals of its Celtic background and inheritance. From this British source it derived very largely the missionary enterprise which became a characteristic feature of Anglo-Saxon Christianity, and enabled the English Church to exercise a reciprocal influence on continental religion and life comparable to that produced in the sphere of material culture from the Bronze Age onwards. Similarly, in the domain of scholarship, it was from the Celtic rather than from the Augustinian tradition that the schools of Anglo-Saxon England and their products drew their inspiration.

The synthesis of the two traditions into a composite whole under the papal jurisdiction was a difficult and delicate task which demanded patience, statesmanship and vision; qualities hardly conspicuous in Wilfrid. By no means all Englishmen shared his admiration of and enthusiasm for Roman usages and decrees, and foreign interference in the affairs of their country was, as it always has been, abhorrent to the British temperament and spirit. There were practical reasons for supporting the Whitby decisions, and these could be bolstered up by theological arguments which in those days seemed convincing enough for the purpose, but they did not override the inborn conviction that however desirable unity of observance in ecclesiastical custom might be, this should not be allowed to conflict with national independence.

Wilfrid was permitted to go to Gaul for episcopal consecration on his nomination to the See of York, but when he elected to prolong his stay abroad for a year, the Northumbrians installed Chad in the bishopric. Therefore, on his return in 666 after a hazardous voyage, which included an encounter with pagans on the Sussex coast, Wilfrid was compelled to retire to Ripon. There he devoted himself to building a basilica of continental architecture with side porches and chapels, and exercised a roving episcopate in Mercia and Kent, founding monasteries and suppressing remnants of Celtic usages.

The Organization and Consolidation of the Church in England

In 668 the Pope at the request of the Kings of Northumbria and Kent appointed to the Archbishopric of Canterbury a continental monk of outstanding ability, relentless energy and profound administrative wisdom, Theodore of Tarsus in Cilicia. The first task of the new Primate was to organize a diocesan system and centralized government of the Church to weld together the heterogeneous collection of communities and institutions which at that time comprised the Church in England. Unwieldy bishoprics extending over large tracks of country had to be subdivided to admit of more adequate episcopal oversight, and if the establishment of the parochial system was much more casual and accidental than has often been imagined, Theodore at least made a beginning of a diocesan organization which eventually was to play an important part in the ecclesiastical administration of the country when the monks withdrew into their monasteries and the bishop occupied the position formerly held in the Germanic civilization by the chief surrounded with his band of companions.

On his arrival in 669 Theodore made a tour of inspection of the existing bishoprics. At Rochester he filled the vacant see and then proceeded to East Anglia to consecrate the new Bishop of Dunwich. On reaching York in the autumn he reinstalled Wilfrid and declared the consecration of the saintly Chad invalid as it was derived in part from the schismatic Celtic succession. To regularize his position he reconsecrated him and subsequently translated him to Mercia making Lichfield the seat of the new see. The following year the first round of episcopal appointments was completed by the establishment of a Bishop of the West Saxons at Winchester instead of at Dorchester, in Oxfordshire, which formerly had been the seat of the see. Having thus brought under his own authority the whole of England on diocesan lines in general conformity with continental practice, he next turned his attention to the establishment of synodical government and legislation, and the introduction of an effective disciplinary system to deal with the many abuses that were rife both in the monasteries and throughout the land.

In 673 he called together the first provincial council at Hertford, composed of all the bishops as a corporate body under his chairmanship in the capacity of Primate of all England: a gathering that has been described by Stubbs as "the first constitutional measure of the English race." (*Dictionary of Christian Biography IV*, p. 928.) At that time the Church was the only representative of the English nation as such, and the unity of the episcopal organization, together with the meeting of the bishops in synods, had a centralizing tendency which prepared the way for the political union of the so-called Heptarchy into the English nation at a later period. Thus, it is significant that such great ecclesiastics of the period as Bede and Boniface speak of their countrymen as the "English" rather than as Northumbrians, Mercians or

West Saxons, although technically the nation only had a corporate existence as a church. The Council of Hertford, therefore, represents a landmark in the development of the English constitution, being a prototype of future Witenage-motes and Parliaments as well as of the Convocations of Canterbury and York. At it it was agreed that the Roman date of Easter should be maintained throughout the land, canonical discipline enforced respecting the rights of each bishop in his own diocese without interference from other dioceses, and monks be prevented from moving from one monastery to another. Reference was also made by the archbishop to the vexed question of the subdivision of the dioceses which were much too large for effective administration. But no decision was reached on this matter.

THEODORE AND WILFRID

The Primate, however, was not the kind of man to be thwarted or delayed in any course of action upon which he had made up his mind. Wilfrid was also equally determined and very jealous of his own position and authority. Therefore, he was not likely to acquiesce in any curtailment of his sphere of unbounded activity in the enormous area he controlled from the Humber to the Firth of Forth. Realizing this, without any consultation with Wilfrid, Theodore proceeded to obtain the consent of the King of Northumbria to divide the diocese into four parts, and forthwith consecrated three new bishops to administer them. Wilfrid thereupon promptly appealed to Rome over the heads of the Archbishop and the Northumbrian King, and without a moment's delay set off for Rome to plead his cause at the fountain head of all ecclesiastical jurisdiction. This raised at once the fundamental issue of the interference of a foreign power in local affairs in England, though it may not have appeared in this light to the impetuous Wilfrid, who certainly displayed no eagerness to return to his northern See. When eventually he arrived back in Northumbria in 680 armed with a papal bull ordering the restoration of his bishopric in its former extent, he found not only that the three new sees were duly filled but that he had himself been sup-planted by a successor as Bishop of York. Neither the king nor the Witan was in the least impressed by the bull, which it was alleged had been obtained by bribery. And so far from his being reinstated in his office and territorial rule, he was put in prison for nine months and then banished from the kingdom. Theodore was content merely to send a statement of the situation to Rome and leave it at that until in 687 the two protagonists were reconciled. Then the archbishop, acting on his own initiative, restored Wilfrid to the diminished See of York.

The first appeal to Rome of an English ecclesiastic, therefore, was ignored in practice by the Church and the secular authority, thereby showing that in the seventh century the country maintained its right to manage its own domestic affairs without let or hindrance from a foreign power, however august might be its spiritual prerogatives. When at a later date, after the death of Theodore, Wilfrid made a second journey to the Holy See to renew his appeal, the Pope, mindful of the fate of the bull of his predecessor, was careful to recommend the settlement of the dispute by an English Synod in accordance with his wishes. There the matter was allowed to rest for the time being, but the Church in England having placed itself under the papal jurisdiction, Wilfrid acted perfectly logically and reasonably in referring his case to the ultimate court of appeal in Christendom. By so doing, however, he began a process that was destined to have far-reaching consequences in the history of the Church and nation when papal supremacy became more definitely and firmly established.

SCHOOLS AND SCHOLARSHIP

A happier outcome of the controversy was the part that it played indirectly in the launching of an evangelistic campaign in Friesland in Holland, where Wilfrid spent some time during his visits to Rome. This enterprise was carried on by a succession of Anglo-Saxon and Celtic missionaries from the monastic schools in the British Isles. As the ancient cultural centre in Northern Europe Ireland led the way, partly no doubt as a result of its contacts with Brittany and the Loire, where the State school survived well into the fifth century. But important as was Ireland, it was only one source of the movement. Both Theodore and his abbot, Hadrian, as Bede tells us, were "well read in sacred and secular literature," and from them flowed "rivers of knowledge to water the hearts of their hearers" whom they daily gathered round them. Trained in the schools of Tarsus, Athens and North Africa, they taught in addition to "the books of Holy Writ the arts of ecclesiastical poetry, astronomy and arithmetic." And in his own day Bede records the existence of scholars who were "as well versed in the Greek and Latin tongues as in those in which they were born."

If this statement is correct, the school of Theodore at Canterbury must have contained pupils unrivalled, north of the Alps, in their linguistic attainments. It is not surprising, therefore, that the institution attracted such notable adherents as Aldhelm, the learned Abbot of Malmesbury, afterwards Bishop of Sherbourne, whose writings had a profound influence on English and continental scholarship for more than a century. Among other products of the famous school were Albinus, from whom Bede derived most of his information about Kentish history, and Tobias, Bishop of Rochester, who is also said to have been a master of Greek.

BEDE

In the north, York and Jarrow were renowned centres of Irish and continental learning associated with the immortal names of Alcuin and Bede. As a lad Bede (673–735) had entered the monastery which Benedict Biscop had established at Monkwearmouth, but a few years later, when Biscop founded a second house at Jarrow, the young Bede was transferred there. The founder was himself a man of considerable learning and a patron of the arts, who had sojourned altogether in seventeen monasteries on the continent to discover all that could be known of the life and ideals of a monk before he returned to Northumbria with builders and glaziers from France. The result of his travels was the erection of simple structures consisting of a small church surrounded by a series of huts or cells for the brethren, who by the middle of Bede's life numbered about 600 in the two monasteries (Wearmouth and Jarrow). The heavy mortality suffered when plague fell

C

on these communities shows that conditions under which the monks lived must have been bad, but spiritually the standard was high in the Benedictine foundations in early eighth-century England. And Bede stands out as one of the finest products of his age.

If he was a monk of simple faith and deep piety, he was also a genuine scholar, and a great teacher who made the glory of God the chief end of existence. While he was uncritical in his use of his authorities, he selected his material with great skill, distinguishing carefully between the transitory and ephemeral and the things of permanent value and significance. Stories of incredible miracles occur on almost every page of his *Ecclesiastical History*, but such events were an integral part of the life and thought of his times. Then men lived in the realm of the marvellous, and holy people who had devoted themselves body and soul to the practice of religion, saw in all the occurrences of everyday life the outward and visible signs of God's presence and power in the natural order and in human affairs. Nevertheless, Bede caught the spirit of the society in which he was born, and unconsciously wrote his own auto-biography in his *History* and his *Lives of the Abbots*. Moreover, when Alfred translated the *Ecclesiastical History* into the vernacular, England had the distinction of being the first nation in Western Europe to have such a record in its own language, and of providing a pattern for all future historians. By going back to earlier sources and collecting his material from ancient documents, he left a storehouse of knowledge for all subsequent generations in which was preserved the local history of his times, literature, prosody, hymnology, astronomy and the *computus*, arithmetic, medicine, rhetoric, the mystical interpretation of Holy Scripture, hagiology and accounts of current theological controversies. In the living Latin of his age he wrote easily and he was also acquainted with the Christian Fathers and the classical poets.

ALCUIN

Although, contrary to various legends, he never left his native land, copies of his works passed to the Continent, but it was through his pupils that his influence was felt even more perhaps than through his writings. By them his fame was carried far and wide, and it was one of his disciples, Egbert, who founded the school at York where Alcuin spent the first half of his life. Having acquired an immense range of knowledge in grammar, the arts and the sciences, at the age of sixty he was invited by Charles the Great to reside at his court and re-establish learning in the Carlovingian Empire. As head of the palace school at Tours, and later of the Abbey of St. Martin, he became the leading English scholar on the Continent, and diffused Anglo-Saxon learning in Central Europe. If he lacked Bede's power of co-ordinating information and added little to the general store of knowledge of his period, he transmitted the teaching of his predecessors and gave to English learning a wider range of influence. All Europe, in fact, was his school and his influence stretched from Tours to Fulda and Rheims, until eventually it was felt in the Universities of Paris and Oxford. Thus, the lamp lit by Bede and Alcuin kindled a beacon in the Dark Ages till the dawn broke in the twelfth century.

THE MISSIONARIES

The evangelization of Friesland begun by Wilfrid also had been carried on by one of his former disciples at Ripon, Willibrord, another Northumbrian destined to diffuse Anglo-Saxon faith and culture among the pagan Germanic tribes. Having become Archbishop of Utrecht, in 719 he was joined by Wynfrith, better known as Boniface (680–754), the apostle of Germany; a Devonian by birth and professed at the Benedictine house at Nursling, in Hampshire. Convinced that his vocation lay among his ancestral Saxons, Boniface refused to succeed Willibrord at Utrecht, and laboured abundantly for the conversion of Hesse in Frankish territory on the borders of Saxony, and then proceeded to Thuringia to effect long overdue reforms there. With the help of English monks he built churches and monasteries, reorganized the Church in Bavaria, and by restoring the papal jurisdiction over this wide area of the Carlovingian Empire, Boniface played a significant part in creating the later idea of a Holy Roman Empire. But important as was his work and influence as an agent of the Papacy, he was essentially the leader of the Anglo-Saxon mission to pagan Germany.

Thus, the British Isles were largely responsible for the dissemination of religion and culture in continental Europe in the Dark Ages and of promoting the Carlovingian Renaissance. Roman civilization was a spent force, and neither the Church nor the Barbarians had any real interest in literature, art and learning, sacred or profane, when these missionaries first appeared on the scene. It had, in fact, become a virtue to renounce scholarship as a relic of the pagan heritage. Outside such centres as Rome, Pavia, Milan, and Ravenna, continental education was at a very low ebb until the new impetus from the North-west brought life and light to a dying and dark age.

THE NORSE INVASION

Strenuous times, however, lay ahead in England. During the lifetime of Bede Northumbria was in a state of downfall and decay, while on the Continent the Saracens had reached the centre of France. But worse was still to come in the British Isles when the whole country was harried by the Vikings, or Nordic adventurers from Scandinavia. At the end of the eighth century the coasts of East Anglia, Wessex and Northern Britain were ravaged, together with the Orkneys, Ireland, Devon and Cornwall. Beginning as sporadic raids for plunder, small colonies soon were established in the north of Scotland and the adjacent islands. Iona was destroyed in 802, and the great monasteries of Northern Ireland with their schools fell during the first half of the century. In England permanent settlements of Danes spread from the Thames estuary and Kent to Mercia, Northumbria and Wessex, until the tide was turned by Alfred the Great when he defeated Guthrum at Chippenham in 878. But the destruction wrought by these invasions hindered the progress of the Anglo-Saxon Renaissance, though they brought about the consolidation of the country as a united kingdom.

In Alfred of Wessex the nation found a new rallying point and the conversion of the Danes to Christianity led to the amalgamation of two races. Although the considerable stores of learning that had been accumulated at Canterbury by Theodore and Hadrian, and in the north by Benedict Biscop and Alcuin, were scattered or destroyed, in due course Alfred was able to revive English letters and to regenerate the national life.

The country, however, was too exhausted to return to its former missionary zeal and the clergy were too illiterate to aspire to learning and culture. Therefore, to fill the restored monasteries the king had to import monks from the Continent until he could raise the general standard of education in England.

Schools were set up and Alfred himself acquired a knowledge of Latin in order to translate into English some of the books which "are most necessary for all men to know."

These included Gregory's *Pastoral Care*, Bede's *Ecclesiastical History* and Bœthius's *De Consolatione Philosophiæ*. To assist him in this work he collected a band of scholars from West Mercia, Wales and Ireland, a priest from the Abbey of St· Bertin in Flanders, and a Saxon monk of Corbey. The *Anglo-Saxon Chronicle* was remodelled and transformed into a national document in English, thereby giving a new impetus to the production of a national literature in the vernacular which became one of the many permanent benefits Alfred bestowed upon the country. From the best editions he could find, those of Inew and Offa, he promulgated a new code of the West Saxon Law, and paid careful personal attention to legislation and the dispensation of justice. But his main interest lay in the revival of religion and learning, though it was not until after his death in 900 that his efforts to reform the monasteries and raise the intellectual level of the clergy were crowned with success.

THE REFORMS OF DUNSTAN

This was accomplished largely through the work of Dunstan, a West Saxon who had become Abbot of Glastonbury, and subsequently in 959 Archbishop of Canterbury. For 400 years the monastic rule founded by St. Benedict at

Monte Cassino in Italy[1] had been adopted by countless communities throughout Western Europe, but although Wilfrid and Benedict Biscop had endeavoured to establish it at Ripon and Wearmouth, it was not until the tenth century that it was put into practice at all effectively. At that time Fleury, in France, was the most powerful centre of the movement, and it was on this model that Dunstan set himself to reform the English monasteries as he had experienced the rule at Ghent during his exile in Flanders. As Abbot of Glastonbury he stiffened the discipline of his Order, and on his preferment to the Primatial See of Canterbury he was instrumental in enforcing the Benedictine mode of life on the older foundations as well as establishing over forty new religious houses, aided by the Bishop of Winchester, Ethelwold, who was an enthusiastic supporter of the movement.

The zeal of the archbishop, however, was not confined to these reforms. Against the drunkenness and immorality of the age he threw the whole weight of his office and personality, and he was equally persistent in his efforts to raise the intellectual and moral level of the parish priests and laity. That he favoured the celibacy of the clergy is beyond doubt, but while he dealt effectively with the anomaly of married men living in quasi-monastic establishments, there is no evidence that he enforced legislation against the marriage of secular priests as such, or compelled every clerk in Holy Orders to put away his wife. However much they might be frowned upon by ecclesiastical authority, clerical marriages in England were common in Saxon times, and even as late as the thirteenth century the practice of universal celibacy was regarded as an innovation, often honoured more in the breach than in its observance.

The permanent value of Dunstan's work is most con-

[1]The Order founded by St. Benedict at Monte Cassino about the year 500 envisaged "a community ruled by an abbot elected by the monks for life, supported by the products of its fields and gardens and having within the wall of its enclosure all that is necessary to convert the produce into food, and to make and repair clothing and other articles of common use." (D. Knowles, *The Monastic Order in England*, p. 4.) Four hours each day were to be devoted to Mass, the saying of the Divine Office, etc., four to reading and meditation, one hour to meals and the rest to manual work, with eight hours for sleep.

spicuous in the contribution he made to the consolidation of the nation and the building up of the shattered ecclesiastical structure on the foundations laid by Alfred. The times required a strong man, and if he was overmasterful, intriguing and sometimes unscrupulous, he gave the lead just when it was most needed. It was unfortunate, however, that when a rude and barbarous age ought to have been subject to the spiritualizing and civilizing influences of religion, his policy tended to separate the cloister from the secular world and its activities.

THE COMING OF THE NORMANS

After his death in 988 the country entered upon a troubled and confused period with Danish invaders struggling for the mastery until in 1041 the English line of the "Redeless" Ethelred was restored in the person of Edward the Confessor. For nearly thirty years this well-meaning but very mediocre monarch had lived in the Norman court. He was himself the son of Emma, daughter of the Duke of Normandy, whom Ethelred had married to establish an alliance with the French province. With England and English ways of life and speech he was completely out of touch, and having nothing but contempt for the barbarous people, as they appeared to him, over whom he had to rule, he filled the court with Normans, Bretons and Flemings. On these he bestowed some of the most important offices in Church and State, though actually the number of Normans among the king's priests was not large. His policy was unpopular however beneficial it may have been to the cultural development of the country by introducing a higher standard of learning and civilized behaviour in a very rude age.

In his personal character Edward was both astute and easy-going, mild-mannered and conscientious, but while he enjoyed the company of cultivated French ecclesiastics, and perhaps adopted celibacy from choice, there is no reason to suppose that his practice of religion attained unusual heights of devotion or asceticism. He may have possessed reserves of latent piety which won him the title of "Confessor," but his clerical appointments revealed little understanding of the spiritual needs of the nation. Moreover, the absence of an heir to the throne raised a complicated constitutional problem. Harold, the son of Godwin, Earl of Wessex, and leader of the English party, after the death of his adventurous father in 1053 was regarded as the inevitable successor by an important section of the nation in preference to the youthful Edgar Atheling, grandson of Edmund Ironsides. It was also alleged that Edward had committed the kingdom to him on his death bed. Therefore, despite an oath to support the claims of William, Duke of Normandy, extracted from him when he was a prisoner in France, Harold assumed the throne at the death of the Confessor in 1066, but only to fall before the Conqueror at Hastings nine months later.

While William met with stubborn resistance, especially in the West Country, the North and the Fens of East Anglia, and only completely subdued all the more important areas of England, the Norman Conquest represents the beginning of a new era for the island. The invaders became the dominant rulers and succeeded eventually in consolidating the country on a feudal basis out of which emerged a composite Anglo-Norman civilization. The existing institutions were brought into closer relation with the secular and spiritual regime of the rest of Western Europe, and at the same time respect was shown for the national traditions and customs where this was practicable under the circumstances.

THE ANGLO-NORMAN CONSOLIDATION

In the selection of the Abbot of Caen as Primate at this critical juncture, William made a wise choice. Lanfranc was a cultivated Italian who had lived in Normandy for most of his life. As Prior of Bec he transformed a small and insignificant Benedictine monastery into a renowned centre of learning before he was transferred to the Abbacy of Caen. On his arrival at Canterbury in 1070 he found the cathedral in ruins, the clergy hopelessly illiterate, the monks lax in their discipline and the general moral and spiritual level of the country lamentably low. The situation may not have been quite as bad as it was represented by the despondent archbishop,[1] but

[1] Cf. R. R. Darlington, *English Historical Review*, 1936, pp. 385ff.

there can be little doubt that the conquest had left a sorry trail of murder, robbery, violence, and a complete absence of moral standards. All this, coupled with the lack of education and cultural amenities, gave a reasonable excuse for the pessimistic attitude of Lanfranc towards the island in which with great reluctance he had been compelled to take up his abode and to determine its destinies as the occupant of the most influential office in the land, second only to that of the Conqueror himself.

Despite his chagrin, he set to work at once to reorganize the Church along the orderly lines introduced by Theodore, and to restore the learning and sanctity that once characterized Anglo-Saxon monasticism. Looking to Normandy for his inspiration and precedents, for him reform meant not so much regeneration from within as the introduction from without of continental methods, standards and order. But if this was to be accomplished he must have an absolutely free hand in the spiritual sphere. This brought him into conflict with the recently appointed Archbishop of York, Thomas of Bayeux, who refused to give a written profession of obedience to the chief see of the Southern Province. William and his Norman advisors gave their support to Lanfranc inasmuch as they realized that the independence of the Northern Province—a region by no means wholly amenable to Norman control—might lead to an independent Archbishop of York crowning a rival king, possibly of Danish or Scottish origin. The Pope thought it politic to leave the matter to be settled locally by the proper ecclesiastical authorities acting under papal commission, and at a synod held at Windsor in 1072 the primacy of Canterbury was confirmed. As at Whitby 400 years earlier, the theological arguments employed to substantiate the claim were as unconvincing as the alleged papal letters were of doubtful authenticity, but although the primacy was not recognized in perpetuity as Lanfranc desired, another step forward was taken in the direction of the consolidation of the hierarchy and its jurisdiction in a single centre which itself was subject to the ultimate control of the Holy See.

Lanfranc, it is true, was not always on the most cordial terms with the Pope, but his respect for papal authority was never in question. Although he opposed interference in matters of episcopal government, provincial organization and administration in local affairs, he supported the papal reforms and relied on papal privileges to justify his claims to the primacy of England. In permitting some relaxations in connection with the vexed question of clerical marriage for instance, he was merely acting in accordance with long-established local custom and from a sense of expediency, not in any anti-papal spirit. Indeed, the Pope himself (Pascal II), in the next century (1107), allowed sons of the clergy in England to hold benefices, and several bishops of Durham, and at least one Archbishop of York, had children. There was, therefore, nothing very revolutionary in Lanfranc's attitude to this difficult administrative problem.

A more crucial issue arose when Gregory VII (Hildebrand), the great reformer of the Church and the real founder of the medieval papacy, demanded that the king should do homage to him and his successors as a papal vassal. To have acquiesced would have meant reducing England to the level of a papal state, and neither William nor Lanfranc was prepared to consider such a proposal for a moment. Moreover, with hostile forces at the very gates of Rome and a rival in the person of Guilbert, the Archbishop of Ravenna, claiming his throne, Gregory was not in a position to take any action in the matter. To have driven the English king and his archbishop into the camp of the enemy would have been fatal at this critical juncture, and so they could and did ignore the appeals of Guilbert and the threats of Hildebrand. To strengthen their position they maintained a neutral attitude towards the two claimants to the Apostolic See, and asserted the Royal Supremacy as the final court of appeal in ecclesiastical administration within the realm.

Church and State constituted a complete whole making for the stability of both disciplines. Therefore, William and Lanfranc respected and understood one another, and recognized the administrations, allegiances and responsibilities in their respective domains. Under their dual control the English Church maintained its prestige and independence, and the Primatial See, assisted by forged letters purported to have been written by Gregory the Great conferring privileges on Canterbury, became virtually a Patriarchate, which embraced Ireland and Scotland. Thus, in 1074, Lanfranc consecrated in London the new Archbishop of Dublin, and at the invitation of Margaret, the Scottish queen, he corrected certain prevalent abuses north of the Border.

INVESTITURES

So long as the two jurisdictions were exercised in harmonious relationship all was well, but with the demise of William, followed immediately by that of Lanfranc, a very different situation arose. As a result of the Norman conquest the Church in England had become feudal rather than national, papal instead of independent. With this twofold allegiance, on the one hand to the king and on the other to the Pope, the spiritual authority was in a very precarious position, especially at a time when land was the chief form of ecclesiastical endowment. In feudal society the act of installation carried with it an acknowledgment that the possession of a property was conditional on the fulfilment of certain duties and obligations to the suzerain who made the investiture. This virtually constituted a relationship of vassal and liege-lord expressed in the act of homage and the oath of fealty symbolized and confirmed by the delivery of certain "presents."

From the beginning of the sixth century the custom had arisen of the Pope conferring upon his vicars and metropolitan bishops a band of white wool called the pallium, originally worn only by himself, as a token of their rank and jurisdiction as head of a province, such as Rome, Alexandria, Constantinople, and later Ravenna. This presentation was extended later to other metropolitan sees of which Canterbury was one and York another. Before receiving the pallium the recipient had to make a profession of obedience and faith to the Pope, and from about 927 Archbishops of Canterbury (and from 1026 Archbishops of York) went to Rome to take the oath of allegiance. Interpreted in the light of feudal custom, this practice gave sovereign rights in a realm in which the papacy claimed sole and universal jurisdiction. Gregory VII was not slow to recognize that if his dream of absolute papal supremacy was to be realized, the investiture of bishops with the insignia of their office by temporal princes must be prevented at all costs. Therefore, he issued decrees against it.

In England the legislation of William I had prevented these decrees from becoming operative, and when he was succeeded by his worthless son, Rufus, the new Primate, Anselm, accepted the ring and staff at the hands of the profligate king and did homage to him without any qualms of conscience. The trouble began with the request of the newly appointed archbishop to go to Rome to receive his pallium from the hands of Urban II, the Pope whom Normandy had accepted as the rightful occupant of the Holy See as against his rival claimant Clement. England being still neutral in the matter of the papal schism, this gave William Rufus his chance to pick a quarrel with Anselm, whom the king had only appointed under the duress of an illness he feared might prove fatal. On his recovery he was determined to wreak vengeance on the learned and pious Primate he had been forced to install after he had kept the see vacant for four years and enjoyed its emoluments.

Anselm may have lacked the personality and administrative capacity of his predecessor, but he had behind him in increasing numbers the barons and the people who were beginning to realize that the Church was the only institution strong enough to defend them against the growing tyranny of royal supremacy. Therefore, in spite of the support of time-serving bishops, Rufus had to acknowledge Urban and agree to the pallium being placed on the high altar at Canterbury by the papal legate, who had brought it to England from Rome, the archbishop himself taking it as from the hands of the Pope. The king, however, only waited his opportunity to pay off yet another score against Anselm, this time selecting the surer ground of infringement of feudal duty in supplying inferior troops for a Welsh campaign. Incidents of this kind, coupled with the deplorable spiritual and moral condition of the court and country, and the deflection of his own bishops, led the harassed Primate to seek the aid of the only authority that could deal with such a situation. So in November, 1097, he set off for Rome to put the case before Urban.

For three years he remained abroad, and during this time he attended a council at the Lateran at which the decrees against lay investiture were promulgated afresh. So impressed was he by this attempt to assert the papal authority in its plenitude that on his return to England after the death of William II he refused to do homage to his successor, Henry I, for the restitution of his temporalities, or to recognize any bishop or abbot who had been invested by the king. In taking his stand on the side of the new (i.e., post Hildebrandine) Roman legislation he departed from the attitude maintained by William I and Lanfranc, which, as we have seen, admitted at any rate some measure of local independence and royal supremacy. Anselm's policy was calculated to transform bishops into papal rather than royal officials, and while in the light of recent experience, this may have seemed to many the lesser of two evils, a considerable section both of the clergy and laity in England supported Henry in his prolonged controversy with the intransigent archbishop, Anselm was regarded with the awe of a saint and respected as one of the most profound thinkers in Europe. This reputation was justified by his piety and great contributions to metaphysical and sacred learning. He failed, however, to understand the inherent insularity of the nation over which he had been called to exercise spiritual jurisdiction and its fundamental dislike of foreign interference in its ancient customs. It was certainly not anti-papal, as subsequent events were to reveal, but it drew a distinction between loyal obedience to the Holy See and its own feudal and legalistic rights as an independent country. The investiture controversy ended in a compromise in which bishops and abbots were to be elected by the respective chapters in the presence of the king and do homage to him, but the bestowal of the ring and staff was to be made exclusively by the spiritual authority. By this arrangement Henry secured the oath of fealty, which virtually made the hierarchy his vassals, and obtained also the renewal of the sentence of excommunication from all persons who had incurred censure during the prolonged struggle. Thus the king got most of what he was anxious to maintain though at the price of surrendering to the Pope a privilege his predecessors had zealously guarded for nearly two centuries. The Church undoubtedly had shown its strength and power to resist effectively royal commands within certain limits but only by the acceptance of the new situation created by the Hildebrandine papal reform movement in which the consolidation and unification of medieval Christendom was vested in the absolute supremacy of the spiritual power centred in the Holy See as the seat of the Vicar of Christ and successor of St. Peter, destined to become *sacerdos imperator*.

BIBLIOGRAPHY

Brooke, Z. N., *The English Church and the Papacy*. Cambridge, 1931. *History of Europe from 911 to 1198*. Cambridge, 1938.

Church, R. W., *St. Anselm*. London, 1888.

Crawford, S. J., *Anglo-Saxon Influence on Western Christendom*. Oxford, 1933.

Hodgkin, R. H., *History of the Anglo-Saxons*. Oxford, 1939.

Knowles, D., *The Monastic Order in England*. Cambridge, 1941.

Laistner, M. L. W., *Thought and Letters in Western Europe*. London, 1931.

Levison, W., *England and the Continent in the Eighth Century*. Oxford, 1946.

Macdonald, A. J., *Lanfranc*. Oxford, 1926.

Plummer, A., *The Churches in Britain before A.D. 1000*. Vol. II. London, 1912.

Robinson, J. A., *The Times of St. Dunstan*. Oxford, 1923.

Stenton, F. M., *Anglo-Saxon England*. Oxford, 1943.

Thompson, A. Hamilton, *Bede: His Life, Times and Writings*. Oxford, 1935.

CHAPTER III

THE CHURCH IN MEDIEVAL ENGLAND

THE consolidation and unification of Western Christendom in the medieval papacy unquestionably produced temporary advantages in a turbulent age of strife and intrigue even though, as will be seen, the institution contained the seeds of its own decay. For roughly a couple of centuries after the death of Gregory VII in 1085, it was the dynamic centre of European civilization, binding together in a great spiritual commonwealth diverse types of race and culture in a common religious and ecclesiastical tradition. Feudalism arising out of a tribal state of social life lacked a centralized authority and relied on the law of force and the right of might. It separated human groups by countless divisions of allegiance and jurisdiction in a multiplicity of lordships with no permanent legislative body, judicial machinery, or political organization. To remedy these defects in the heritage from Teutonic barbarism and Celtic tribalism, a wider conception of citizenship was needed with deeper loyalties overriding all distinctions of class and nation.

It was this that the medieval Church supplied with its own constitution and culture, its own law and sovereign head who claimed and maintained as of divine right supreme and absolute authority in matters spiritual and temporal. And it cannot be denied that at the height of its achievement in the thirteenth century it produced one of the greatest ages the world has ever known, despite so much that was radically wrong with the system and its institutions. To this period we are indebted for such masterpieces of architecture as Westminster Abbey in its present form, and the magnificent cathedrals of Amiens and Chartres, of Salisbury, and the superb Angel Choir at Lincoln. Among men of learning, letters and genius, the names of St. Thomas Aquinas, Grosseteste, Dante and Roger Bacon are outstanding figures, while in St. Francis of Assisi the new spiritual culture of Western Christendom reached its climax in devoted service to God and his fellow men for Christ's sake. It was at this time of great intellectual activity that the universities grew and began to make their influence felt, supplemented by the educational work of the grammar schools attached to cathedrals and collegiate churches under the jurisdiction of their chancellors, the friars' schools, and those belonging to the religious houses. Moreover, bad as conditions were in many departments of secular and ecclesiastical life, serious efforts were made to remedy some of the most conspicuous scandals urgently calling for reform.

In the eleventh and twelfth centuries the revival of Western Europe began under papal leadership as a result of the Hilde-brandine movement. In England the quarrel between William II and Henry I, on the one side, and Anselm on the other, turning chiefly as it did on the two rival claims to supremacy and sovereign jurisdiction, came to a head in the reign of Henry II. Assertions of papal authority were inherent in the collection of Canon Law which Lanfranc introduced and made the basis of the Canon Law of the Church of England, but the ancient native customs established by William I acted as an effective barrier against undue interference on the part of the Holy See, apart from these written codes. Nevertheless, in the troublous days of the civil war between Stephen and Matilda, when the king himself referred his case and cause to the judgment of Rome, much ground was lost to the papacy. To redress the balances and reduce the turbulent barons to order, Henry II realized the urgent need of a strong central government. If this was to be accomplished he must obtain control over ecclesiastical appointments and remedy the flagrant abuses of the "privilege of the clergy" in the trial of criminous clerks in the Church courts. Thus, during the first nine years of his reign more than a hundred murders had been committed, it was alleged, by persons who claimed to have received the tonsure, and so were exempt from civil legislation.

The "Privilege of the Clergy"

To appreciate the significance of the situation it has to be remembered that in medieval England probably about one in twelve of the adult male population of the country was for practical purposes a "clerk in Holy Orders" in the sense of being a tonsured person.[1] Many of these had no intention ever of doing priestly work of any kind, and, of course, had no vocation, and had had very little education or training for their office. None the less, they could claim the "privilege of the clergy" and the right to be tried in the ecclesiastical courts for all crimes except high treason and certain very minor offences. Furthermore, all that was required to establish their claim was to be able to show that they were wearing a tonsure. This situation, needless to say, led to every kind of abuse and Henry was perfectly right in his endeavours to deal with it.

The death of the Archbishop of Canterbury, Theobald, in 1161 gave him his opportunity to appoint a successor who would carry out the necessary reforms, and in the selection of his trusted friend and jovial companion, Thomas Becket, he seemed to have found the man of the hour. As Chancellor he had proved himself to be an invaluable ally, and it could hardly be doubted that he would be an equally staunch and faithful Primate. But Becket was the perfect actor who lived his part in whatever role he played. Possessed of a dominant personality, he made firm friends and fierce enemies, and whatever he undertook he did thoroughly, whether it were hawking, riding, administering the affairs of State or those of the Church. Consequently, as soon as he found himself duly installed as the head of the Church in England he adapted himself to the new character he embodied as completely as when he acted as chancellor. And it is to his credit that he had warned the king that he would bitterly regret his choice if he insisted on making him Archbishop of Canterbury. "Love," he said, "will turn to hatred."

At his consecration the new Primate saw a vision of himself as the leader and champion of the spirituality against royal encroachments and feudal suzerainty arising out of the Carlovingian Empire. And Henry was not long left in doubt that his former protégé and ally had become his resolute

---

[1] To arrive at anything approaching an accurate estimate of the actual figures is impossible because not only are the ordination lists very incomplete but many were admitted to minor orders (acolytes, subdeacons, etc.) who never proceeded to the priesthood though they claimed the privileges of the clergy.

D

opponent. Resigning the chancellorship and assuming the great black cloak of the Augustinians with the cowl of the Cistercians, Becket set to work to recover the alienated property of his see and to throw the whole weight of his office against the attempt to restore the ancient customs in force before they had been modified by the new papal supremacy movement. These royal demands were embodied in the form of written constitutions drawn up and published at Clarendon, in Wiltshire, in 1164, and included among other provisions that clerks accused of any crime having been summoned by the king's justiciar, after conviction were not to be protected by the Church in the ecclesiastical court. Furthermore, appeals were to go from the archdeacon to the bishop and from the bishop to the archbishop, but no further (i.e., to Rome) without the king's leave. Bishops and archbishops and other dignitaries were also forbidden to quit the realm without the royal consent.

All this was little more than the codification of the ancient usages as they had prevailed in England since the days of the Conqueror, and even the claim that degraded clerks should be tried in the secular courts, though, as Becket maintained, involving a double sentence, was not unknown on the Continent. But the controversy turned on the deeper issue. The question at stake was whether or not the Roman legislation of the reform movement was to prevail in England. The archbishop was determined that it should, and for good or ill the tendency of the age was against a return to the pre-Hildebrandine situation. In the popular mind the papacy stood as the bulwark against royal and imperial tyranny, and notwithstanding Becket's gross infringement of the rights of the laity, he became the personification of the rising tide of public opinion.

That he deliberately precipitated the crisis that raised him to the altars is apparent, but in anticipating martyrdom and canonization he played his final role with great skill and conspicuous success. Nothing could have been more dramatic, and in the twelfth century better calculated to bring about the desired result than his spectacular demise at the hands of "the king's men" in his own cathedral. Such a death was sure to produce a legend and a cultus, and to bring his adversary to his knees as a penitent before the shrine of his erstwhile enemy, now hailed as a saint. And the Pope was not slow to seize the heaven-sent opportunity and turn it to his own ends. With the scattering of the brains of the archbishop on the pavement of the chapel of St. Benedict at Canterbury, the Constitutions of Clarendon were shattered at a single blow. Henceforth it became impossible to prevent appeals to Rome or to bring a tonsured clerk to justice in a civil court, except on a charge against the forest law, despite the ever-increasing abuse of "the privilege of the clergy," until nearly 400 years later the nation was compelled to reverse the judgment it had passed on the royal supremacy as a result of the murder in the cathedral on that grim and foreboding afternoon of the 29th December, 1170.

THE STRUGGLE FOR ENGLISH LIBERTIES AND REFORMS

The Roman Canon Law now became operative in its entirety in England without let or hindrance from the king's authority, and more decretals were addressed to this country by Alexander III than to all the rest of Europe. The numerous appeals to the Holy See show that the English episcopate relied increasingly upon the papacy in their local administration though in spite of Canon Law archbishops continued to consecrate to vacant sees after homage had been done to the king for the temporalities. Furthermore, the papal legates were required to obtain royal consent before entering the realm. But resistance to the demands of Rome was very difficult, and it only remained for a weak and vacillating monarch like John to pit himself against an Innocent III to reduce the throne to the status of a papal vassal. Nevertheless, Stephen Langton, the Pope's nominee to the Archbishopric of Canterbury, endeavoured to maintain the liberties of the land so far as it lay in his power, and in conjunction with the barons, it was under his influence that Magna Carta was drawn up and sealed at Runnymede on 15th June, 1215.

This declaration of English liberties, however, did not at all fit into the policy of Innocent who promptly annulled it, excommunicated the barons who had signed it, and suspended Langton for refusing to publish the excommunication. The death of both the Pope and the king (John) the following year brought the dispute to an end and the Charter was confirmed at Bristol in the presence of the legate. This laid the foundation of the liberties claimed and in a measure enjoyed by the English nation ever since. The principle of self-taxation by national consent inherent in Magna Carta as against the feudal practice of payment to the king in lieu of military service, gave the executive a powerful weapon against royal sovereignty, and played its part in the establishment of parliament by Edward I as a representative assembly with its members drawn from the boroughs sharing the legislature with the knights of the shires. In this achievement the Church took its share, and in the struggle led by Simon de Montfort the indefatigable Bishop of Lincoln, Robert Grosseteste, was a prominent figure.

FARMING BENEFICES

The whole of the episcopate of this remarkable Englishman was one continuous contest against abuses in Church and State. He was born of peasant stock in Suffolk about 1175, and after learning Greek and Hebrew during his academic career at Oxford and Paris, he became a scholar of repute alike for his "excellent wisdom and most lucid power of teaching as well as a pattern of all virtue." Soon after his consecration to the See of Lincoln in 1235 he made a personal visitation of his diocese to obtain first-hand knowledge of the condition of the parishes. This revealed the widespread custom of farming out benefices so that the rector, who was frequently an Italian nominated by the Pope, made an arrangement with the abbot of the local monastery to receive the tithe, pay him as non-resident rector a fixed sum annually and make the monks responsible for the ministrations of the parish. An alternative method was for the monastic house to pay a given amount to the rector and recover it with interest from the emoluments of the benefice, the monastery getting the work done as cheaply as possible by a priest acting as vicar. This iniquitous system was also resorted to by pay patrons who had inherited advowsons attached to their estates. To correct what he described as the "degradation of the free bride of Christ into a position of slavery," Grosseteste struggled to secure the institution of vicars responsible to the bishop for the care of the parish and paid a fixed income out of its revenues. At length, despite bitter opposition from interested parties, such as the Templars and Hospitallers, he obtained papal consent and authorization for the reform, but not before he had carried the war into the citadel of the Roman *Curia* and in the presence of Innocent IV, with the vigour of a Hebrew prophet, denounced it as the seat of all the evils from which the Church of the period was suffering. Nevertheless, he was an uncompromising supporter of the Hildebrandine reform movement, believing that papal sovereignty made for righteousness, though he was always ready to take his own line as and when occasion required. Thus, he refused to institute the Pope's nephew, Fiderigo di Lavagna, to a canonry in his cathedral, showing "as an act of filial reverence" that the candidate was quite unfit to hold the office. Similarly, on his return to England in 1252, he withstood in Parliament the demand of the king (Henry III) for a tenth of all ecclesiastical revenues to finance a crusade.

CLERICAL INCOMES

Since the fourth century tithe had been paid to the clergy as a moral duty based on Old Testament precedents, and in England in 787 its payment was made compulsory by law. With the development of the feudal system after the Norman Conquest all ecclesiastical property was regarded as sacred and belonged to the spirituality, at the head of which stood the papacy.

The bishops held lands direct from the Crown and let them out to knights and others in return for revenues and services rendered. Parish priests also were in a feudal relationship with their bishop who demanded canonical obedience from them as a condition of institution to a benefice and the enjoyment of its emoluments. The bishop in his turn was bound to protect his clergy and their freeholds against lay interference, though the lord be the patron of the living. The Pope as the Vicar of Christ exercised unquestioned supremacy, and, therefore, when he required funds for a crusade, or holy war anywhere, he levied a tax on the country, the burden of which fell heavily on the clergy because they belonged to the spirituality and had to contribute to papal needs from the emoluments of their benefices.

An assessment of clerical income for this purpose, commonly known as the "Norwich valuation" since it was prepared by Walter Suffield, Bishop of Norwich in 1254-5, including as it did glebe, tithe, offerings in kind and perquisites, throws light on the financial position of the clergy in the thirteenth century, though unquestionably it very considerably underestimated the values of benefices. Thus, in the dioceses of Lincoln and Norwich, seventy-four vicarages were assessed at a total of 669 marks whereas the register of Hugh de Walles, Bishop of Lincoln, gives a total of 1,009 marks. These discrepancies led to a reassessment in 1266 "according to the true value and not according to the ancient estimation." This increased the levy by 33½ per cent, while a subsequent valuation in 1276 to raise funds for a crusade, doubled the Norwich figures despite the bitter opposition of the clergy. In 1288 the gift of a tithe by Pope Nicholas IV to Edward I towards another expedition to the Holy Land in which the English king took part, led to the assessment of 1291-2, which remained the basis of all ecclesiastical valuations until the Reformation. They were still actually below the real revenues in many cases though occasionally the position seems to have reversed the *taxatio*, giving higher figures than those of the documents.

But making due allowance for these discrepancies, it is clear that the medieval clergy in England were by no means a wealthy body. The number of parishes in the country in the Middle Ages is difficult to conjecture, but apparently it ranged from between 8,000 and 12,000, with an average population of 300.[1] Of these, except for a few very rich benefices, such as Lindisfarne and Bambridge, both estimated at over £250 (i.e., about £6,000 in modern currency), and at the other end of the scale some amazingly poor livings like Tamerton, in Devon, assessed at 3s. 4d. (i.e., £4), £10, or £240 in our values, probably represents approximately the annual value of the majority of parishes, though incomes often

[1] Even in the few towns that existed, the parishes were exceedingly small, seldom rising above about 200 in population.

must have fallen well below this average. Therefore, it is not true to say that the secular medieval clergy as a body were over-paid. Indeed, when it is remembered how many benefices were "farmed out" by non-resident pluralists, the lot of the vicars, who acted as their deputies, was not an enviable one, compelled as they were to eke out an existence on a mere fraction of the official emoluments. Moreover, out of the gross total the charges on the living have to be deducted, and these seldom amounted to less than about £5 per annum (£100) spread over curates, church cleaners, pensions, payments to the bishop (synodals) and such-like charges.

The monasteries, it is true, were potentially wealthy, having become large landowners, and so far had the original ideal of voluntary poverty been abandoned as an integral part of the religious life that not only abbots and priors but monks in general were to all intents and purposes men of very considerable substance, of which the medieval equivalent of an income of £1,000 per annum would be a conservative estimate. Nevertheless, there was scarcely a monastery in England in the thirteenth century that was not seriously in debt, largely owing to the gross mismanagement of its estates by incompetent abbots and bad business methods. It was only because they had behind them such vast resources that most of the houses were able to survive at all when they fell on hard times arising out of the vicissitudes of farming, fluctuations of the wool industry, the devastating effects of floods, murrain and fires, and the burden of papal and royal taxation, in addition to their own incompetence.

THE EPISCOPATE

Similarly, in the case of the episcopate, while the emoluments of English bishoprics were enormous, ranging from those of Winchester amounting to some £200,000 per annum in modern currency to the modest £4,392 in the case of Rochester, the expenses involved were even more immense, often rendering the diocesan insolvent. Thus, Winchester had no less than fifty manors all of which had to be maintained and staffed together with a huge permanent household, which included chaplains, squires, servants, pages, clerks or secretaries, estate managers, stewards, bailiffs, foresters, fowlers, accountants and auditors. For the medieval bishop was a feudal lord and a principal officer of the State as well as a spiritual pastor. He might, in fact, be Chancellor or Treasurer of the Crown, or a temporal ruler of his territory, devoting himself almost entirely to secular functions.

As he travelled from manor to manor either on state or ecclesiastical business a considerable proportion of his retinue had to move with him, carrying its own food and equipment with it as no manor could provide for the needs of the company when the bishop took up his abode temporarily there for a few days or weeks during a visitation. The records of the household expenses of Richard de Swinfield, Bishop of Hereford, 1283–1317, show that during a tour of his diocese lasting 296 days his household, consisting of forty men and the same number of horses, moved no less than eighty-one times. The amount of food consumed at festivals when he entertained on a large and incredibly lavish scale, is amazing. On Easter Day 1290, the guests, who can hardly have exceeded a hundred, were provided with $1\frac{1}{2}$ carcasses of salt beef, $1\frac{1}{2}$ carcasses of fresh beef, 5 pigs, $4\frac{1}{2}$ calves, 22 kids, 3 fat deer, 12 capons, 88 pigeons and 1,400 eggs, 11 sextaries (i.e., about 66 gallons) of local wine and beer *ad lib*. Well may the editor of the record comment, "so much for the first release from Lenten diet." But hospitality given on this scale was ruinous for the host, and in the ordinary course of his episcopal duties he was expected to lead a peripatetic existence with no really permanent abode and this regiment of retainers constantly to feed, clothe and pay. Therefore, though ostensibly wealthy the bishop was generally in financial straits, overburdened with the intricacies of Manorial administration, feudal rights and executive responsibilities as Magistrate, King's Counsellor, and Member of Parliament, apart from his diocesan, ecclesiastical and any other official offices he might hold.

Under such conditions and handicaps that some bishops were students and, as in the case of Grosseteste, Stephen Langton, John Peckham and Robert Winchelsey, found time to write as well as to read books, is surprising. These, of course, were the exception, as only men of the phenomenal energy of

Grosseteste could hold synods and administer effectively their dioceses extending over very large areas,[1] translate large tomes from Greek into Latin, make notable a journey to Lyons to address the Supreme Council of the Church and manage his own financial affairs. Therefore, it is not surprising that many less stalwart members of the episcopate found all their time and resources occupied with their temporalities and in practice became primarily landowners, officers of the Crown, or local magnates, just as monasteries tended to concentrate upon the management of their estates. Visitations were held from time to time by most diocesans, but in the larger dioceses such as Lincoln, Lichfield and York, no bishop with the means of transport at his disposal in the Middle Ages, could visit every parish however diligent he might be. And if he confined his functions to those of a legislative officer, as was the custom, many places escaped episcopal oversight. This may in part account for the prevalence of neglect and even of vice, brought out in the inquiries made at the time of a visitation.

PARISH PRIESTS AND THE COLLEGIATE CHURCHES

The parochial clergy, drawn largely from the peasantry, for the most part were illiterate. Living like the rest of their ancestral stock in rude cottages with little or no furnishings, a complete absence of books and a lack of domestic amenities, there was no inducement to rise to a higher cultural level than their parishioners. They were supposed to say Mass daily and to encourage the laity to attend on Sundays and Holy Days of obligation, and priests were urged to meet together for the corporate recitation of the Divine Office where circumstances permitted. Their work consisted almost exclusively of giving the sacraments to the sick and the whole and the catechizing of children, but preaching was very rare until the influence of the friars revived the practice in the parishes in the fourteenth century. Thus, so long as their priestly functions were confined to a routine of more or less impersonal ministrations, with the possible exception of giving counsel occasionally

[1]The diocese of Lincoln, for example, comprised eight counties distributed between the Humber and the Thames, an area now divided into five separate sees. In the Middle Ages England and Wales contained only twenty-one dioceses against the forty-nine of to-day.

to penitents in the confessional, they were content to devote themselves at other times almost exclusively to the cultivation of their land. In work, dress and behaviour, in fact it was often difficult to distinguish them from their parishioners. Celibacy, as we have seen, frequently was a nominal observance, if indeed any attempt was made to conceal the relationship that existed between the rector or vicar and the woman who lived in the parsonage. So that priest and people, living on much the same level, tended to conform to the standards of their age.

In passing judgment upon the medieval clergy, however, account must be taken of the circumstances under which they had been ordained and in which they exercised their functions. A very large proportion sought Holy Orders for utterly wrong motives, and were given little or no preparation for their office. Most of them were so illiterate that Archbishop Peckham declared that their ignorance "casteth the people into the ditch of error." Having no cultural background or interests, and living in isolation in remote rural districts, they were cut off from any elevating influences. Too many were deputies of non-resident rectors or canons who paid them such a miserable pittance that they were compelled to live a hand-to-mouth existence. Thus, the prebendaries of the great collegiate churches or minsters, such as Beverley, Ripon, or Southwell, farmed out their benefices in the same way as they appointed vicars-choral to take their places in the choir of the minster. The underpaid hirelings could scarcely be expected to take a very high view of their office and functions under conditions of this kind. Moreover, the system had an equally disastrous effect on the collegiate bodies and the chapters of secular cathedrals (York, Lincoln, Salisbury, Wells, Hereford, Exeter, Chichester and St. Paul's in London)[1] inasmuch as it destroyed their common life and the *raison d'être* of their establishment.

In the monastic foundations (e.g., Durham, Canterbury, and Winchester) where monks took the place of secular canons, the corporate life was preserved since the cathedral body

[1]Although the secular cathedrals were sometimes used as parish churches their chapters were not responsible for parochial cures.

continued to live in community under their abbot and their own prior in a joint relationship to the bishop of the diocese, which was not always very clearly defined or easily adjusted. In the early Middle Ages the monastic clergy for the most part were devoted men who fulfilled their rule in an edifying manner until they too became corrupted by the accumulation of wealth. The appropriation of parish churches to religious houses made the monks responsible for the provision of local ministrations. But this readily conflicted with their monastic vocation, its discipline, functions and corporate life. Therefore, they had to provide deputies whom the bishops rightly insisted should be given a fixed income and security of tenure of the benefice they held from the monastery. By the thirteenth century the practice of monks acting as parish priests was almost unknown, if it ever obtained to any extent. A few regular (i.e., monastic) canons served a group of parishes, but the normal custom was to delegate parochial work to secular vicars and chaplains who received not more than a third of the income of the benefice. A further drain on the resources of the parishes came from the provision of pensions for members of the religious communities with which they were associated.

THE FRIARS

Taking the evidence collectively, we are left in no doubt that in the thirteenth century the time was ripe for a new conception of the religious life (i.e., the monastic vocation) and the recovery of spiritual ideals on the part of the Church and the clergy as a whole. This crying need was supplied by the movement initiated by two outstanding figures of the period; namely, St. Francis of Assisi and St. Dominic. Both recognized the failure of the existing orders and the secular clergy to fulfil their proper mission in the world and attain the ends for which they should be striving. St. Francis saw the remedy in a vision of the poor preaching the Gospel to the poor in a life of humility, simplicity and renunciation. To this end he collected round him a devoted band of Grey Friars content to beg their bread and dwell in the most squalid quarters of the towns as they made their way across Europe as itinerant mendicants, until they reached England in 1224. To the vagabonds and outcasts of society they primarily directed their message of salvation, despised learning and culture, and almost made a fetish of ignorance, poverty and simplicity.

St. Dominic and his Black Friars, on the other hand (who preceded the Franciscans by three years in their arrival in England in 1221), realized that more learning rather than less was the urgent need of the times to combat the heresy that was springing up on the Continent, and the prevailing illiteracy of the English clergy which made it impossible for them to vindicate the faith effectively. In England lethargy, ignorance and pluralism rather than heretical beliefs were the outstanding evils, and in this country the work of the Dominicans lay in raising the intellectual standard of the Church and nation. Already, however, a beginning had been made in the establishment of an important centre of sacred and secular learning at Oxford in the latter part of the previous century, followed in 1209 by a second foundation at Cambridge. Here lay a rich field for the activities of the Black Friars, and under the influence of Grosseteste the Franciscans were induced to abandon their original attitude towards scholarship and become a learned order. The change, however, had a profound effect upon the earlier ideals of the Grey Friars, who in settling at Oxford and devoting themselves to intellectual pursuits were compelled to modify very considerably the ideals of absolute poverty and itinerant mendicancy inculcated by their pious founder. Indeed from glorying in ignorance they rapidly became the most learned order of the age and produced the greatest scholars in England in the thirteenth century, e.g., Roger Bacon, John Peckham, William of Ockham and Duns Scotus.

The Universities

Gradually the influence of the universities was felt in the parishes as more and more graduates were ordained to benefices, though their number remained relatively small. In the archdeaconry of Stow, for example, between 1235 and 1253 Grosseteste instituted thirteen incumbents who had taken a master's degree, and this was a high percentage due in part no doubt to the fact that Oxford then was in the diocese of Lincoln and its bishop was an enthusiastic scholar himself. However, the fact that these men had studied the seven liberal arts, divided into the *trivium* (grammar, rhetoric and dialectic), and the *quadrivium* (arithmetic, astronomy, music and geometry), and lived in the atmosphere of a university, meant that they were educated men who gradually would leaven the illiterate lump.

As in the present school of *Literae Humaniores* (commonly called "Greats") at Oxford, which in some measure is based on the medieval curriculum, there was a combination of the classics with philosophy (i.e., grammar with dialectic) in the arts course. And as the thought of the Middle Ages developed under the powerful stimulus of the scholastic movement, dialectic acquired an increasingly dominant position in the universities.

It was, however, from the side of logic and theology that medieval learning derived its inspiration. Logic raised the perennial problem of "universals," or the way in which the particular parts of a thing are related to a certain group of objects as a composite whole, and the determination of the element that gives them individuality and makes them the source of knowledge. The ramifications of this abstract problem ranged over a very considerable portion of the philosophical field of inquiry and led to an investigation of the ultimate nature of universal concepts and of individual objects of perception in the real world. Moreover, it had its bearing on the theological situation since, interpreted ecclesiastically, the universal Church was the absolute reality, particular things (such as individuals and national churches) having reality only in relation to the whole, unified in the papacy. At the top stood the Pope as the representative of the Church universal, and in a graded hierarchy of authority the several parts were absorbed in the entire organization, i.e., the Holy Catholic Church, outside the jurisdiction of which particular or national groups could have no valid existence, any more than individual human beings alone are real. It was not until the Middle Ages had come to an end that a new scientific spirit arose which destroyed the former solidarity of thought as well as of organization, and made individual things virtually the only realities. With the break-up of the absolute sovereignty of the papacy as a fact, the individual and the nation came into their own as independent entities. In the Middle Ages there was no suggestion of such a disintegration.

The medieval approach to theology was conditioned by the rediscovery of Aristotle through the impact on the Western mind of Greek philosophy introduced by the Arabs. From the early Christian Fathers the Church had inherited an enormous mass of sacred learning, and the systematic organization of this material, begun by Anselm and Abelard, reached its climax in the magnificent philosophical synthesis of St. Thomas Aquinas. Hitherto the Latin West had been cut off from the Byzantine East and knew little of Greek thought except through Latin translations of some of the Greek Fathers, and the works of the Neoplatonist known as the Pseudo-Dionysius. It was not until the ancient Hellenic philosophical literature was made available in the twelfth and thirteenth centuries that a new phase of Western theology emerged, strictly orthodox and conservative in spirit and outlook, but alive to the new movements of speculative thought and mystical experience that had penetrated Europe at the beginning of the Middle Ages. In the capable hands of Bonaventure (1225–74), Albertus Magnus (1206–80) and Thomas Aquinas (1223–74) a remarkable synthesis of knowledge was built up and critically examined by Duns Scotus (1270–1308) and William of Ockham (c.1280–1347). Thus, the older Augustinian tradition was intermingled with Aristotelianism to produce the three great medieval systems in which faith, reason and theology, and philosophy were brought into an harmonious relationship, while St. Bernard combined mystical inward experience with the ascetic austerity of monasticism.

At Oxford the new movement was encouraged and developed by Grosseteste and the Franciscans he established there. The Dominicans would have been a rather more obvious choice since they were essentially the learned order by their constitution whereas the followers of St. Francis were evangelists. Actually the Preaching Friars (Dominicans) in England did not find very much scope for their particular mission because heresy has made no headway in the country, and in scholarship they were unable to compete with their Franciscan rivals. If both had worked together in their respective spheres they might have succeeded in arousing the Church from its spiritual lethargy. Instead the friars quarrelled with each other, and with the secular clergy whose rights they failed to respect in the matter of hearing confessions, the burial of the dead, and, like Wesley and his followers in later times, preaching in the parishes with scanty regard for the jurisdiction of the local incumbent. Nor were their relations happier with the monasteries, for not without reason the monks saw in the new movement a challenge to their own established position and way of life. The genuine asceticism of the original mendicants was a reproach to the laxity of the regulars of the old foundations, and with the growth of friaries, funds were diverted from them to the rapidly increasing new religious houses. Thus, by the end of the thirteenth century there were fifty-one Dominican houses and fifty-five Franciscan friaries in England, making a total of not less than 5,000 friars in the whole country.

THE DECLINE OF THE MEDIEVAL CHURCH

The rapid decline of this very considerable force from the lofty ideals that inspired the movement in its early stages was a potent cause in the general decay that set in at the end of the Middle Ages. The abandonment of mendicancy was accompanied by a growing laxity in the observance of the rule of the orders and a display of wealth and luxury completely out of keeping with the high standards of austerity maintained in early days. Similarly, the monks from being the most respected section of the spirituality had steadily deteriorated in discipline, influence and numbers, until by the fourteenth century they were as spiritually bankrupt as their monasteries were insolvent and falling into ruins. Many of them were saddled with pensions called "corrodies" for officials and servants who continued to reside in them after their retirement from active work, or who demanded board and lodging in exchange for land or monetary advances. The multiplication of chantries in private houses, churches and cathedrals created an unedifying class of Mass priests whose only duty it was to say or sing Requiems daily for the repose of the soul of the founder in return for a small benefaction. Then came the "pardoners," or hawkers of indulgences, equipped with spurious relics and a host of superstitions.

Behind this age of decay lay the disintegration of the unifying centre of Western Christendom. The papal supremacy having been bolstered up by forged decretals, solemnly pronounced as authentic and authoritative by Gregory VII, now presented to the world the unedifying spectacle of two infallible jurisdictions, each fully equipped with a constitutionally elected occupant of the Chair of St. Peter and a conclave of cardinals, excommunicating the supporters of its rivals and waging wars described as crusades against its opponents. This state of affairs inevitably raised very serious theological problems as well as practical questions of policy at a time when a new national consciousness was springing up everywhere. That the institution weathered the storm is a remarkable testimony to the hold that it had on the allegiance of Europe. But it opened the way for reformers like Wyclif (c. 1328–84) to question the validity of the papal claims, while the attempts to heal the breach by the decisions of General Councils, although abortive in their results, raised the all-important question of the relation of the Pope to the Church of which he was the head. National jealousies proved to be too strong to force an issue, and from the struggle the Holy See emerged triumphant. Nevertheless, the Avignon "captivity," and the subsequent Great Schism, mark the beginning of the end of the medieval papacy. The spirit of self-assurance so conspicuous in the new series of Renaissance Popes, as evidenced, for example, by the Inquisition, represents the pride that so often precedes a fall.

England for the most part stood outside these stirring events on the Continent, and whatever anti-papal feeling there was in the country was directed towards interference with national rights and the prevalence of ecclesiastical corruptions. There was certainly no theological revolt. Thus, when Wyclif attacked the accepted doctrine of transubstantiation and the spiritual authority of the Pope, he lost popular support and it only remained for him and his followers, the Lollards, to be branded as heretics and social revolutionaries, to prevent the movement becoming a serious challenge to the stability of the Church and nation. Moreover, if the dignitaries, monks, and friars had lost the respect they previously enjoyed, the parochial clergy in the fourteenth and fifteenth centuries were a new rallying point. Thus, it was upon the parish churches, now erected in the perpendicular style, that the laity concentrated their resources, especially in East Anglia, where some very fine buildings made their appearance at this period.

The regenerative movements, therefore, of the great thirteenth century lived on in this English counterpart of the Renaissance in Italy and Germany, but the paganism that followed in the wake of the continental New Learning never reached the British Isles. Its influence here was felt mainly among devout churchmen like Archbishop Warham, Dean Colet and Sir Thomas More, while at Oxford the movement was fostered by patrons of Greek scholarship—notably by Humphrey, Duke of Gloucester—while William of Wykeham in founding Winchester and New College had been careful to associate sound learning with religion. It was this principle that differentiated the English Renaissance from its continental counterparts and prevented a pagan reaction to the excessive medieval scholasticism that hitherto had prevailed in the principal intellectual centres. Thus, on the eve of very great and fundamental changes in the religious thought and practice of the country, there was little deep-seated discontent with, or probably not much interest in, the prevailing theological position. Apart from Lollardy, the temporal authority and spiritual primacy of the papacy seemed to be as firmly established at the beginning of the sixteenth century in England as it was during the Middle Ages.

BIBLIOGRAPHY

Bennett, R. F., *The Early Dominicans*. London, 1937.

Brooke, Z. N., *The English Church and the Papacy*. Cambridge, 1931.

Cutts, F. L., *Parish Priests and their People in the Middle Ages in England*. London, 1914.

E

Dawson, C. *Medieval Religion*. London, 1934.

Gasquet, F. A., *Parish Life in Medieval England*. London, 1906.

Gibbs, M., and Lang, J., *Bishops and Reform, 1215-72*. Oxford, 1934.

Gilson, E., *The Spirit of Medieval Philosophy*. London, 1936.

Knowles, D., *The Monastic Order in England*. Cambridge, 1941. *The Religious Houses of Medieval England*. London, 1940.

Little, A. G., *Studies in English Franciscan History*. London, 1917.

Lunt, W. E., *Valuation of Norwich*. Oxford, 1926.

Moorman, J. R. H., *Church Life in England in the Thirteenth Century*. Cambridge, 1945.

Offer, C. J., *The Bishop's Register*. London, 1929.

Owst, G. R., *Preaching in Medieval England*. Cambridge, 1926.

Parker, T. M., "Feudal Episcopacy" in *The Apostolic Ministry*. Ed. K. E. Kirk. London, 1946.

Powicke, F. M., *Stephen Langton*. Oxford, 1928.

Powys, A. R., *The English Parish Church*. London, 1930.

Rashdall, H., *The Universities of Europe in the Middle Ages*. New edition by F. M. Powicke and A. B. Emden. 3 vols. Oxford, 1936.

Smith, C. M., *Pre-Reformation England*. London, 1938.

Stevenson, F. S., *Robert Grosseteste*. London, 1899.

Webb, J., *A Roll of the Household Expenses of Richard de Swinfield During Part of the Years 1289-90*. Camden Society. 2 vols. 1854-5.

CHAPTER IV

THE ENGLISH REFORMATION

AT the beginning of the sixteenth century the reaction against medieval culture and religion was an established fact. The papacy it is true was intact, but even in the Latin South the Middle Ages were regarded as "a dark age of Gothic barbarism," while in Northern and Central Europe a new force was about to arise which would hail it as a time of degradation and superstition; the reign of antichrist. Moreover, the prolonged struggle between spiritual and temporal rulers, and the resultant schism in the supreme sovereignty of the Church and its visible head, coincided with the growth of a new nationalistic consciousness which found expression in a desire for ecclesiastical reform. The Spanish kings, for instance, took the matter into their own hands and after a wholehearted repression of heresy, dealt effectively with corruptions and abuses in their own realm, and then extended their efforts to the papal court itself. The French monarchs, not content with asserting their independence, claimed as part of their treaties a measure of control over the Pope himself. In Germany pluralism and the sale of indulgences were rife, and the phenomenal success of Luther's crusade shows that it only required the striking of a match to set the country alight as a beacon of the Reformation.

THE CONDITION OF PRE-REFORMATION ENGLAND

In England the situation was less tense than in the rest of Northern and Central Europe. Relative isolation from the turmoil of the continental papal sovereignty, coupled with the protective legislation that had become firmly established with many vicissitudes since the Norman Conquest, modified very considerably the tyrannies and corruptions of the mainland, where the Pope was little more than one of the warring Italian rulers dependent for support on one or other of his patrons. In its theological outlook and allegiance the country, as we have seen, was solidly Catholic, and in its struggles over investitures, "the privilege of the clergy," appeals to Rome, papal provisions and *praemunire*, and the validity of bulls and licences, were merely expressions of intense local patriotism devoid of any fundamental doctrinal significance. The spiritual prerogatives of the Holy See were never in question, nor were their underlying claims disputed. It was accepted, in fact, because it represented a supramundane absolute authority, standing outside the temporal order by virtue of its Petrine heritage. As such it was regarded as an effectual check on royal despotism as well as the guarantee of an ultimate standard in faith and morals. It was only on the lower plane of temporal jurisdiction that a conflict between Church and State was always liable to arise, and what happened in the twelfth century in the relations between Alexander III and Henry II, or between Innocent III and John in 1213, was repeated 400 years later when Henry VIII became involved in a dispute with Clement VII over the king's domestic affairs. But this time the royal will prevailed with far-reaching consequences for the subsequent history of the Church in England. Nevertheless, it is important to remember that the English Reformation began as an episode in the age-long conflict between Church and State and not, as in Germany and Switzerland, in a theological revolt against Catholic doctrine and discipline. In England this came later.

Henry VIII succeeded where Henry II failed because the medieval unity already had been disrupted. England in the meantime had become more firmly established as an independent and self-supporting country, and the Crown assumed greater prominence as the pivot of national consciousness. The Renaissance papacy was less deeply rooted in English soil than its medieval predecessor; the discovery of new worlds was giving a wider geographical outlook, and the New Learning was directing thought and culture away from the theological interests of scholasticism and fostering a more critical attitude towards the established order everywhere. Moreover, this new spirit of independence had already produced a breach in the papal solidarity of Northern Europe with the rise of national churches in Germany and Switzerland which had repudiated its authority. At such a time under the prevailing circumstances, a contest between Church and State might easily become a permanent schism. And this is what occurred in the sixteenth century in England.

On the surface Henry's request for the nullification of his marriage with Catherine of Aragon might appear merely as yet another bid for "insular independence" on the part of a headstrong monarch, determined to have his way in a sordid matrimonial adventure. Numerous precedents could be quoted for papal dispensations from matrimonial cases, as when Louis XII married Ann of Brittany, the widow of his brother-in-law, during the lifetime of his lawful wife. At her death he contracted an alliance with Henry's youthful sister, Mary, and Mary at his death married the Duke of Suffolk, who had also taken a third wife by dispensation during the lifetime of her predecessor. But special care had been taken to regularize the marriage of Henry VIII with the widow of his brother Arthur by a dispensation from Julius II in 1503, reinforced by a solemn declaration on the part of Catherine that the union with Arthur was never consummated. Therefore, apart from the fact that the all-powerful nephew of the queen, the Emperor Charles V, was active at Rome on behalf of his aunt, it would not have been easy for the papal lawyers to have discovered an adequate cause for annulment.

THE BREACH WITH ROME

Henry, however, was quite determined to have his way, and if the Pope could not be induced to nullify the marriage, the only course open to the king was to repudiate the jurisdiction of Rome in the realm. Therefore, fortified by a vote against the dispensation of Julius II by the universities, secured through the intervention of Thomas Cranmer, Henry boldly declared himself "supreme head of the Church of England," and assumed full control of all ecclesiastical authority in the country, despite the opposition of the clergy. In Cranmer, however, he found a ready accomplice, and as soon as he was appointed to the Primatial See, the tacit consent of the spirituality was obtained under threat of *praemunire*.[1] Nevertheless, that it was necessary to invoke this stern threat in order to secure the acquiescence of the clergy, shows that the English Reformation did not arise as an anti-papal popular demand for reform and schism on the part of the Church, as in continental countries. Rather was the breach forced upon a reluctant hierarchy and a bewildered nation to meet the royal demands, which incidentally were not unconnected with the absence of a legitimate male heir to the throne.

Once, however, the schism was an accomplished fact by the excommunication of Henry in 1533 and the proclamation of the Royal Supremacy, the divorce became merely an incident in a much wider and deeper issue. The latent reforming tendencies soon took shape, and while Henry remained consistently and persistently Catholic in his theology and practice (as might be expected in one who had received not without some reason the title of *Fidei Defensor* for his refutation of the sacramental teaching of the German reformer, Luther) there were other very different forces at work within and without the country which speedily began to make their influence felt. The growing spirit of nationalism and the weakening of papal authority had opened the way for a new bid for royal supremacy on the part of the king, while the insipient Lollardy going back to the crusade of Wyclif and the Peasants' Revolt in the previous century, joined with other anti-clerical movements at home and abroad, to create an atmosphere favourable for reform of a more drastic character than was contemplated or tolerated by Henry.

THE SECULARIZATION OF CHURCH PROPERTY

The stand made on behalf of the retention of the ancient papal jurisdiction was surprisingly small once the breach with Rome had been made, being confined for the most part to the Carthusians and men of sound learning such as Fisher,

---

[1]This was the name given to statutes passed in 1353, 1365 and 1393 to prevent suits being carried outside the realm to the court of Rome, and the bringing into the land of any documents, bulls or sentences of excommunication prejudicial to the rights of the Crown or his realm, on pain of forfeiture of lands and imprisonment; cf. W. T. Waugh, *The English Historical Review*, April, 1922. Vol. XXXVII, pp. 173-205.

Bishop of Rochester, and Thomas More. This is partly to be explained by financial causes and partly by the lead given by the new Archbishop, Cranmer, supported by Latimer, Bishop of Worcester, Shraxton of Salisbury and Foxe of Hereford, and a strongly anti-clerical House of Commons. In 1535 Thomas Cromwell as Vicar-General visited churches, religious houses and the clergy to collect information with a view to the secularization and confiscation of their property and the dissolution of the monasteries, notwithstanding their renunciation of the papal authority. The treasury needed their potential resources, and the way had been prepared by the seizure of monastic lands and revenues in previous reigns to meet current requirements.

That the religious orders were in urgent need of reform is beyond dispute, but their total suppression without any attempt at rectifying the abuses cannot be justified on these grounds, nor was reformation the motive of the dissolution. In the first place it was not easy to fit them into the new ecclesiastical order, and the reorganization of the diocesan system required new bishoprics and additional suffragans. To finance these sees—Westminster, Gloucester, Oxford, Chester, Peterborough and Bristol—some of the monastic revenues were used, while abbots and priors were made deans of the foundations transformed into secular cathedrals—Durham, Rochester, Winchester, Ely, Norwich and Carlisle. The monks were installed in benefices or retired on pensions, and the advowsons formerly owned by the monasteries were acquired in many instances by private patrons. Nevertheless, after deducting these transferences of Church property to new beneficiaries, the balance on some £50,000,000 (in modern values) seized by the Crown was very considerable.

Although the number of religious (i.e., monks and nuns) who refused to acquiesce in this wholesale destruction of their vocation was surprisingly small, and the actual martyrs negligible,[1] the secularization of the orders was by no means popular in the country. The rebellion in the North, known as

[1] The most notable resistance was at the London Charterhouse in 1534 and its sequel in the barbarous executions at Tyburn. The Abbots of Reading, Glastonbury and Colchester were also hanged and mutilated.

the Pilgrimage of Grace, was an indication of the resentment felt by a considerable section of the people, especially of the lower classes, not only at the suppression of the lesser monasteries but of the general trend of events. This doubtless would have become an irresistible movement on a national scale if it had not been that the changes in faith and practice were relatively slight. But if Henry had no wish or intention of producing a doctrinal reformation when he broke off relations with Rome, and had nothing but contempt for continental Protestantism, he had been manœuvred into an impossible position theologically. An unkind fate had driven the erstwhile Defender of the Faith into the camp of his German opponent. Faced at any moment with a threatened papal crusade against England, Henry could not afford to isolate himself completely from continental alliances and influences, and his separatist policy compelled him willynilly to look in the direction of Lutheran Germany for support. Moreover, he was surrounded with prominent administrators who were Lutherans rather than Catholics at heart. Therefore, as the reaction against the old ecclesiastical order grew in the country, it was only a matter of time before it was given visible expression in doctrine and discipline.

Nevertheless, the king was determined not to make more concessions than he could help, and in 1536 Ten Articles were drawn up in which the faith of the Church of England was enunciated in terms of the traditional sacraments of Baptism, Penance and the Eucharist in combination with the Lutheran doctrine of justification by faith, a repudiation of indulgences and a restatement of the doctrine of the Real Presence. The next year the teaching of this document was expanded in the "Institutes of a Christian Man," or "The Bishops' Book," in which diverse uses of national churches were justified. But Cromwell and the Lutheran Party had little support among the clergy or laity outside London, and with a political change in the continental situation a reaction set in against the reformers.

To restore the position a new set of Six Articles was promulgated in 1539 affirming the doctrine of transubstantiation, the practice of giving Communion in one kind only and of saying private Masses, the celibacy of the clergy and auricular confession. The "whip with six strings" fell heavily upon the Lutheran party. Cromwell followed More and Fisher to the Tower, Cranmer survived but his power passed into the hands of Gardiner, Bishop of Winchester, Tunstall of Durham, Bonner of London and the Duke of Norfolk. The Bishops' Book was revised in 1543 to make transubstantiation more explicit, and when the king died four years later it is true to say that in outward appearance at any rate England was as Catholic as on his accession.

The Growth of Protestantism in England

The schism, however, had opened the flood gates when the torrent was running so swiftly on the other side of the Channel that it was only a matter of time before the entire country was inundated by the rising tide of Protestantism. Cranmer, in fact, had been employing his comparative seclusion with the preparation of a scheme of drastic changes in public worship and its doctrinal background, and as soon as Henry's disastrous reign ended in 1547 he was ready to put his plans into operation. Meanwhile the continental Reformation had begun to split up into warring sects with Lutherans (or "Protestants" as they were called) occupying a relatively conservative position theologically in Germany and the Scandinavian countries in the Baltic area, and with more extreme elements in the ascendant in Switzerland and Central Europe. These again were subdivided into the followers of Zwingli in Zurich, a contemporary of Luther, and those of John Calvin in Geneva.

The Zwinglians having repudiated uncompromisingly the traditional conception of the Eucharistic sacrifice and the real presence, they substituted Bible expositions for the offering of the Mass and the recitation of the divine office, and began a campaign for the abolition of images, relics, monasteries and Catholic ceremonial. But even these wholehearted innovations did not satisfy a radical and socialistic section of the movement known as Anabaptists, who regarded as anathema infant baptism, a State connection, and every vestige of the traditional faith and practice of Christendom. When the civic authorities took action against them many of them were driven out of Zurich and became a thorn in the flesh of the Reformers all over Northern and Central Europe.

The cleavage between Zwinglians and Lutherans occurred along similar lines. Unlike Zwingli Luther was prepared to retain everything in the old order that did not conflict with his own particular doctrine of justification by faith and the all-sufficiency of scripture as the basis of Christian belief and practice. But many in Germany as well as in Switzerland accepted the more radical attitude of Zwingli and his followers, and as their movement spread through France to the Netherlands it made itself felt in England. Meanwhile in Geneva in 1541 Calvin had gathered his forces in defence of his doctrine of Predestination as opposed to the Lutheran contention of free grace, and of a Church confined to an elect company of believers. Against both Lutherans and Zwinglians the Calvinists maintained that the sacraments were external signs by which Christ sealed on the human conscience His promises of goodwill towards man, to sustain the weakness of faith. As appendages to Holy Writ they were like seals affixed to diplomas and as such were symbols and confirmations of the promises revealed in the Gospel.

Thus, on the Continent the Reformation had begun to display a sectarian character before the death of Henry VIII, and already Zwinglians, Anabaptists and Lutherans hated each other more than they disliked the Church. The Calvinists stood apart from these factions in dignified seclusion as the "Reformed Church" *par excellence*. In England the reforming party at first was mainly Lutheran in tendency but Cranmer soon veered towards the Zwinglian position during the lifetime of the king (Edward VI), though he was always unstable in his opinions and unable to arrive at or maintain consistent convictions of his own, especially in the interpretation of sacramental doctrine. This was at once his strength and his weakness in an age of rapidly shifting scenes and allegiances. When in 1547 Edward VI came to the throne at the age of nine, power passed immediately into the hands of the reforming movement, headed by the compromising Somerset as Protector and the vacillating Cranmer as Primate. Lutherans and Zwinglians poured into the country from all quarters, and before the end of the year Bucer, a Lutheran from Strasbourg with strong Zwinglian tendencies, had been appointed Regius Professor of Divinity at Cambridge, and Peter Martyr Vermigli, an Italian refugee from the Inquisition, to the corresponding chair at Oxford. These, with many other foreign divines, inflamed the reforming zeal of the archbishop with the result that during the five years of the reign of the Protestant son of Jane Seymour (hailed as a new Josiah) the character of the Church in England was completely changed. Beginning with the abolition of candles in churches except before the Blessed Sacrament, the singing of the litany in procession and the restoration of the chalice to the laity, there followed in quick succession the suppression of all surviving chantries, the blessing and distribution of ashes on Ash Wednesday and of palms on Palm Sunday. Then came the institution of an "Order of Communion" in English as an addition to the Latin Mass on Easter Day, 1548, collected mainly from a Lutheran service book known as the Consultation of Hermann of Cologne, drawn up by Bucer and Melanchthon. This represents the first draft of a new Book of Common Prayer, the full text of which appeared in the following year.

THE ENGLISH PRAYER BOOK

However novel it may have seemed at that time to give Communion in both kinds, the custom was merely a return to ancient custom and was not in itself heretical, especially as it was expressly stated that the Host contained the whole body of Christ. Similarly, the First Prayer Book of Edward VI issued in 1549, retained the structure of the medieval Mass, with collects, epistles and gospels taken mainly from the missal of the diocese of Salisbury (Sarum), which had become virtually the normal liturgy in England in the later Middle Ages. The traditional vestments were retained, but while the presence of a congregation was contemplated other than those who had assembled for the purpose of receiving Communion, a new emphasis was laid on reception of the sacred elements by insisting that there should be some communicants at every Mass. The Mass of the Presanctified was omitted from the services for Good Friday, together with the rest of the Holy Week ceremonies, and those of Candlemas and Ash Wednesday. Morning and evening prayer were very much simplified forms of the medieval breviary offices of Mattins, Prime, Terce, Sext, None, Vespers and Compline, with the substitution of a strictly Biblical lectionary for lections chosen partly from the canonical Scriptures but largely from apocryphal and legendary sources.

Despite its moderation, the new Book of Common Prayer was not at all favourably received by either the Henrician or the Reforming parties, or, indeed, by the general public. It contained too many Catholic features to satisfy the Lutherans and Zwinglians, who complained that "the ceremonies and form of administering the Holy Eucharist scarcely differed from those observed in the celebration of the Catholic Mass." This was done, it was said, "that the people might not think anything of the latter had been removed or cut away, but should believe that what had formerly been read in Latin was now being read in English." Actually, however, there were Lutheran tendencies in the new rite which did not escape the notice of those who were determined to maintain the theological position of the previous reign. Thus, all the Henrician bishops voted against it, except Gardiner who was in prison. To secure their support certain alterations were made to strengthen the Catholic trend, and eventually it was accepted without enthusiasm and imposed by statute.

If theologians felt it was capable of a Catholic interpretation, this was sufficient reason for the Reformers to regard it with grave suspicion and even abhorrence. Calvin, for example, denounced the book and the policy that lay behind it, as "puerile and frivolous," and Bucer and Fagius poured forth vituperations on the retention of the Eucharistic vestments, the use of candles on the altar, the chrism at baptism and the commemoration of the dead in the canon. Hopper decried it as "in some points plainly impious" and urged that it should be revised. In the West Country, on the other hand, bitter complaint was made that a religion that was "200 years old" had been radically changed without consultation with the bishops. Open revolt broke out with the passing of the Act of Uniformity in 1549, enforcing the new Prayer Book throughout the land. The re-enactment of the Six Articles was demanded together with the celebration of the Mass in Latin "as it was before without any man or woman communicating with the priest." The blessing and distribution of ashes and palms were to be restored together with all other ancient ceremonies, and the monasteries re-established. To all this Cranmer replied with scorn and derision, but Somerset, with more forbearance and insight, issued a peaceful remonstrance to the rebels.

The fall of the Protector (Somerset) a few months later removed his moderating influence, which was largely responsible for the compromise that found expression in the First Prayer Book of 1549. His successor, the worthless Warwick, proved to be a veritable Rehoboam, as devoid of religious convictions as of ethical values. It suited his purpose to espouse the Protestant cause though on the scaffold he declared himself always to have been a Catholic. In any case, whatever his private beliefs may have been, his policy afforded the opportunity for a revision of the book and the elimination of most of the surviving elements of the old religion. The medieval service books were destroyed, churches were stripped of their ornaments, statues, stained glass windows were broken and treasuries ransacked. A new "Order for the administration of the Lord's Supper or Holy Communion" was drawn up in which the altar was transformed into a table standing in the body of the church as in continental Protestantism. The balance nicely maintained by Somerset was now heavily weighted on the Reforming side where Calvinistic influences predominated. The Canon of the Mass was dislocated by the Communion immediately following the Prayer of Consecration, thereby removing the sacrificial memorial of the Eucharistic offering, the *Agnus Dei*, and the co-mixture of the Host in the chalice, while the "fraction" (or breaking of the priest's host) was to be made at the recitation of the words of institution. The *Gloria in Excelsis* was placed at the end of the service instead of in its original place as a hymn of praise at the beginning of the rite, and the Mosaic decalogue substituted for the nine-fold *Kyrie* before the collects. Wafer bread no longer was enforced, new words of administration were inserted, and subsequently an unauthorized rubric printed in heavy black type (and, therefore, commonly called the "Black Rubric") was added which denied the doctrine of the Real Presence.

As ordered by the new Act of Uniformity issued in March, 1552, the revised services required very few ornaments. This afforded an excellent reason for the collection of valuable plate, vestments, hangings and other spoils from parish churches and cathedrals to replenish the royal treasury, "inasmuch as the king's majestie has need of money." In the same year (1553) Edward died, and, therefore, the Second Prayer Book of 1552 never received the sanction of Convocation. Before the drastic changes were enforced at all effectively, Protestantism suffered a complete reverse with the accession of the daughter of Catherine of Aragon. The foreign divines, including Peter Martyr, and shiploads of their followers, returned whence they came having been provided with passports by the new queen, Mary Tudor, who began her ill-fated reign with marked toleration.

THE REACTION UNDER MARY TUDOR

Nevertheless, if Edward was represented by the Protestant Reformers as a second Josiah, raised up to drive away the false doctrines and practice of a degenerate Catholicism, Mary may well have regarded herself as a divinely appointed Joshua called to power to bring her people from the wilderness of heresy and schism into their rightful inheritance from which they had been excluded by the breach with Rome. Such at any rate was the task to which she devoted herself with an ever-increasing zeal as the conviction was borne in upon her that all the misfortunes of her unhappy life were the judgments of heaven for the heinous sin of schism. Her position manifestly was one of extreme difficulty, though on her accession she received the support of the vast majority of the nation, particularly as regards the religious issue. Her political opponents were discredited as a result of the futile conspiracy in favour of Lady Jane Grey and the fall of Northumberland

Warwick). Elizabeth, her younger sister, the daughter of Ann Boleyn, alone remained as a possible rallying point for Protestant intrigues and a reminder of the need for caution in the restoration of the old faith.

After all that had happened since 1543 when the country first repudiated the papal jurisdiction it was too much to hope that the *status quo* could be restored by parliamentary legislation and royal pressure. The Reformers might be unpopular in many directions, but fundamental changes had taken place not merely in the outward forms of religious parties and factions but in the entire mental outlook of the people. Sacred things were the burning topics of conversation everywhere, in the highways and hedges, the taverns and inns, as well as in the higher counsels of the nation. This endless discussion which was stirring the minds of men and women in half the countries of Europe was destroying the former solidarity and unquestioned acceptance of the established Catholic way of life. The general public, it is true, was not interested in the current theological controversies in their more abstract aspects, but their repercussions on current events became disturbing elements in private life and in the life of the community as a whole. Moreover, there was a widespread feeling of uncertainty. As Professor Powicke says, in the sixteenth century, with the exception of Cranmer, nobody really was very sure what the Church of England was (*The Reformation in England*, p. 33). In this state of confusion Mary had the advantage of the return of the tide towards a shore which was that of a familiar country with a firm anchorage available, and in spite of all the unsettlement, and partly because of it, if she had steered the ship more skilfully, taking careful note of the rocks around her, she might have succeeded in attaching it to its former moorings.

Englishmen had been ready to do without the Pope but they were less inclined to change their customary beliefs and modes of worship. And the schism with Rome certainly had not brought greater peace and harmony to a distracted country. Protestantism, so far as the masses were concerned, appeared in the light of a foreign importation alien to the national tradition. The unheaval during the Edwardian Reformation had been sufficient to produce a reaction in favour of the old régime, with or without the Pope. By her fatal policy of ruthless suppression and persecution, coupled with her unpopular alliance with Philip of Spain, Mary, however, succeeded in reversing the position. The English have never been a persecuting people, and as soon as the queen abandoned her initial tolerance in favour of the mistaken and depraved notion that an *auto-da-fé* was required as a holocaust to expiate the sin of schism, she transformed a country which was fundamentally Catholic at heart into an outpost of the Protestant Reformation. Cranmer, Ridley and Latimer, and the rest of the host of martyrs who perished at her hands, lighted a candle that has never been extinguished. Indeed, the fires she kindled to consume heretics burnt into the very soul of the nation a horror and disgust which it would seem has become a permanent trait in the national character. At any rate, England has never since abandoned its fear of and reaction against Roman Catholicism, and anything it interprets as savouring of "Popery."

THE ETHNOLOGY OF THE REFORMATION

Temperamentally and ethnologically the inhabitants of the British Isles are of composite stock made up of a mixture of round-headed people whose original home was in the Alpine region of Central Europe, and a similar strain from the Mediterranean area in the south, intermingled with long-headed Nordics from the Black Sea and the Baltic. It is significant that at the Reformation the round-headed (or brachycephalic) extravert Alpines and Mediterraneans, among whom the herd instinct is strong, remained Catholic while the long-headed (or dolichocephalic) northern introverts, with their intense individualism, readily adopted Protestantism. In the Alpine region many different stocks fused, but broadly speaking, the Reformation predominated in the northern section of the country while Catholicism prevailed in the south. In England, as we have seen, the numerous invasions and large-scale infiltrations from the Mediterranean and the Atlantic coasts of the Iberian peninsula and France, which played such an important part in the development of English civilization from Neolithic times onwards, have introduced a basic southern strain in the population, overlaid by subsequent Alpine and Celtic immigrations.

This may throw some light on the medieval background of the Reformation and the persistence of a Catholic tradition in England throughout the turmoil in the rest of Northern and Central Europe, to say nothing of the Catholic revival in the nineteenth century. But there is also a very definite Nordic strain in the population going back to the influx of the Beaker Folk (cf. pp. 15) and the subsequent migrations from Scandinavia and the Low Countries, the Middle Rhine, the Elbe and Western Germany; extending from the prehistoric battle-axe cultures to the Norse and Danish invasions in the Anglo-Saxon period. This too has left its mark on the English temperament and religious outlook, affording a predilection for the qualities which emerged in Protestantism, notably north of the Border. In Ireland, on the other hand, the Mediterranean influences predominated. The Beaker Folk never reached its coasts, and the later Norse invasions were only sporadic. Therefore, except in the north where Scottish and Nordic elements prevailed, Protestantism has made little headway. The Marian reaction in England brought out the deeply laid instincts of this Nordic-Protestant element, and once this was accomplished any hope of the establishment of one all-embracing national religion was doomed to failure in the long run.

THE ELIZABETHAN POSITION

It was with this highly complex religious, social, racial, temperamental and political situation that Elizabeth and her advisors were confronted when she ascended the throne in 1558. The offspring of the fatal marriage that had been the occasion of the Henrician Schism with the Papacy, the new queen could hardly be expected to continue the policy of the daughter of Catherine of Aragon. But to precipitate a quarrel with Rome involved the risk of French and Spanish intervention at the very moment when a serious rival in the person of Mary Queen of Scots, granddaughter of Henry VII, and wife of the Dauphin, awaited her opportunities north of the Border,

F

where her marriage had brought France and Scotland into a new alliance with each other and the Holy See. In England, on the other hand, the fires of Smithfield, the loss of Calais, and the Spanish influence at court, were crying aloud for redress, and the group of intimates around Elizabeth left little room for doubt which side she would favour. But at the same time she was not anxious to provoke hostility at Rome. Therefore, she must not make any open move against Catholicism lest she antagonized the Spanish King, Philip II, on whom she depended to prevent a French attack on England when the country was wholly unprepared to meet it.

These were the considerations governing Elizabeth's policy, and she played her hand with consummate skill. On her accession she forbade any changes in religious practice and continued herself to hear Mass according to the Latin rite in her own chapel. But this was only a temporary measure and soon she gave indications where her true sympathies lay. On Christmas Day she deliberately left before the elevation of the host as a protest against an act which was at that time associated with the doctrine of transubstantiation, while two days later she issued a proclamation permitting a partial use of English in the services but forbidding preaching and teaching to avoid agitation from either side. Encouraged by these favourable signs, the exiled Reformers hastened back to England, and those who had been imprisoned by Mary at home began to be released. But although the tide which had brought back the country to its papal moorings had now turned again, the queen had her hand on the wheel and was quite determined to steer her course with care and deliberation, ever mindful of the rocks and quicksands that lay ahead.

In re-establishing the royal supremacy she discarded the contentious title "Supreme Head of the Church" for "Supreme Governor," a designation that implied an administrative rather than an initiatory authority, and gave the Church jurisdiction in matters of faith. But the right of any foreign power to have superiority over her subjects was categorically denied, thereby virtually settling the question of the papal supremacy. In 1559 she called together her advisors to produce a "device for the alteration of religion." It is possible that it was Elizabeth's intention to revive the First Prayer Book of Edward VI, or at any rate to make it the basis of a new revision, but if the returned exiles were to be placated, the Second Book, issued in 1552, must be taken as the model. This gave a Protestant form to the liturgical structure, and when the Forty-two Articles issued at the end of Edward's reign were restored virtually unchanged though reduced to thirty-nine, there was the same emphasis in the sphere of doctrine. The Black Rubric, however, was deleted and the words of administration from the 1549 liturgy were prefixed to those of 1552. Proper lessons for holy days were also appointed and provision was made for Rogationtide processions. But the most significant concession to Catholic practice was the inclusion in the new Act of Uniformity of a rubric declaring that "such ornaments of the Church, and of the ministers thereof, shall be retained, and be in use, as was in this Church of England by the authority of parliament in the second year of the reign of King Edward the Sixth" (i.e., 1549). If this injunction had been carried out, as in fact it is in the great majority of Anglican churches and cathedrals to-day, in outward appearance the services would have been comparatively little changed. But, nevertheless, the structure of the rites resembled the Protestant rather than the Catholic model, while the ecclesiastical constitution remained essentially medieval.

THE ELIZABETHAN SETTLEMENT

Needless to say this compromise really satisfied nobody though it represented a brave attempt to combine in one comprehensive liturgical "settlement" ancient and medieval, Lutheran and Zwinglian elements expressed in the magnificent language of the period and adorned with Catholic ceremonial. At that time, of course, it had not dawned upon anyone that there could be more than one religion in a country, and that by law established. Therefore, the only available method was to make the formularies as vague and non-committal as possible in the hope of embracing within them all and sundry. But after all that had happened since 1553 it was courting disaster to levy a fine of a shilling for non-attendance on Sundays at a composite rite which had been compiled and authorized without even consultation with Convocation, and after nine lay and nine spiritual peers had voted against the innovations—the bill being carried in the Lords by only three votes.

To the Marian episcopate the compromise appeared to abolish "the doctrine and form of religion" in which "our fathers were born, brought up and lived," and to put in their place "something lately brought in, allowed nowhere, nor put in practice but in this realm only; but a small time, and against the minds of all Catholic men." To the more advanced Reformers even the 1552 Prayer Book was equally abhorrent having been devised, according to John Knox, the leader of the Genevan Calvinist school in Scotland, "rather for the upholding of massing priests than for any good instruction which the simple people can receive thereof." Nothing short of the elimination of the entire Catholic structure, organization, faith and practice of the Church sufficed to satisfy the demands of this section. Thus, with two diametrically opposed groups at either end, and a very uneasy and uncertain middle, the Elizabethan establishment was in a precarious condition.

In her choice of a Primate the queen showed the brilliant statesmanship she so often displayed in the many troubled and complex situations which confronted her almost at every turn. The one thing, however, upon which she and her ecclesiastical advisors appear to have been quite resolute was the maintenance of the continuity of the Apostolic ministry whatever else might be abandoned. Up to this point the question of the episcopal succession had not become acute since the pre-Reformation hierarchy remained more or less intact, the Henrician bishops having been appointed and consecrated for the most part before the schism. At the beginning of Elizabeth's reign, on the other hand, all the sees became vacant through death or deprivation except Landaff and Sodor and Man. To some of these the returning exiles were appointed —Grindall, Cox, Jewel and Sandys—but the crucial test of the queen's insight into the needs of the hour lay in the selection of Matthew Parker for the exacting office of Primate. In him were combined the qualities most needed if the settlement was to be put into operation. Against his own wishes he was persuaded to consent to election and on 17th December, 1559, he was consecrated according to the new ordinal in the chapel at Lambeth Palace by Barlow of Bath and Wells, Hodgkin of Bedford (both of whom themselves had been consecrated according to the pre-Reformation rite), Scory, ex of Chichester and elected to Hereford, and Miles Coverdale of Exeter.

The extreme care taken to secure a valid election of Parker and the proper quorum of bishops to raise him to the episcopate[1] at a time when so few Anglican bishops were available, shows the importance attached to historical continuity by Elizabeth and her counsellors, in the spirit of the preface to the Edwardian ordinal, where it is affirmed: "it is evident unto all diligently reading Holy Scripture and ancient Authors that from the Apostle's time there have been these Orders of Ministers in Christ's Church: Bishops, Priests and Deacons. Therefore, to the intent that these Orders may be continued, and reverently used and esteemed, in the Church of England, it is requisite that no man (not being this present Bishop, Priest or Deacon) shall execute any of them, except he be called, tried, examined and admitted, according to the form hereafter following."

It was this insistence on episcopal ordination and government that constituted the main cause of opposition to the Elizabethan Settlement on the part of that section of the reforming party which had adopted the Calvinistic, Zwinglian and Lutheran conception of the ministry, with its repudiation of the Apostolic Succession and all that this involved. Parker, nothing daunted, laboured to create an establishment at once Catholic and Reformed, grounded on the ancient episcopal structure and organization handed on through the ages from Celtic times, when the ecclesiastical order was independent of the Papacy but constitutionally orthodox and valid. Having secured this principle of continuity in structure, the new archbishop made no attempt at any far-reaching schemes of reform. Canons were promulgated to deal with questions of discipline requiring immediate attention, but considerable latitude was allowed in the interpretation of the official formularies (e.g., the Thirty-Nine Articles), and only a small

[1] For an examination of the validity of Parker's consecration see C. Jenkins, *Journal of Theological Studies*, October, 1922, pp. 1-33.

proportion of the clergy refused to conform to the legal requirements demanded by the government. Indeed, in view of the
composition of the Elizabethan spirituality, comprising secular
priests and religious of the Henrician and Marian periods,
returned Protestant exiles, and the general body of the clergy
with varying histories and attitudes towards the rapid changes
that had occurred during their lifetimes, it was manifestly
impossible to require or enforce anything more than nominal
allegiance to the *status quo* in any direction. Moreover, in
dioceses ranging over immense areas, the bishops could not
know what was happening in every parish, and that many
irregularities occurred is beyond doubt. In a few instances
exiles and others exercising Reformed ministries, with or without episcopal consent, were admitted to benefices carrying a
cure of souls (as distinct from such sinecures as cathedral
prebends, deaneries, etc., which did not necessarily involve
the performance of priestly functions), as in the case of John
Morison, Hadrian Saravia, and Whittingham, but they were
isolated irregularities in contradiction to the official policy of
the Church.

Thus, the learned Hooker, Master of the Temple, was
only prepared to condone any departure from episcopal
ordination when circumstances urgently demanded ministrations and no bishop was available, or in the exceptional case
of men raised up directly by God for some special purpose.
Similarly, the Calvinistically-minded Archbishop Whitgift
represented to the queen that Walter Travers was not eligible
for appointment to the Mastership of the Temple on the
ground that he had gone to Antwerp to minister to a private
congregation there in order to escape ordination, "the laws
of the realm requiring that such as are to be allowed as
ministers in this Church of England should be ordered by a
bishop."

Nevertheless, the Elizabethan Settlement failed because its
underlying motive was political rather than religious. Primarily
it was a means of giving stability to the State, and it did not
take account of the insoluble nature of important elements in
the compound that made up the establishment. At the beginning of the reign there were not less than 200 recalcitrant

clergy (known as "recusants") who refused to abandon allegiance to the papal jurisdiction, and probably this number can be increased. After the death of Mary Queen of Scots, who was their rallying point, and the excommunication of Elizabeth in 1570, they became an "underground movement" of potential martyrs trained and reinforced at Douai, in France, by the newly-formed Society of Jesus. By 1580 they claimed to have made 140,000 converts, and although this represents only a small minority of the population it reveals the existence of a vigorous and heroic campaign.

On the other side, the radical Reformers, or Puritans as they were called, were openly hostile and much more numerous. Not being proscribed, they were able to entrench themselves in important positions in Church and State, in the universities and the Inns of Court, and make their influence felt as a powerful opposition. Thus, they became strong enough to prevent the Ornaments Rubric being adhered to in the conduct of public worship, even in its minimum requirements; refusing to wear a surplice or rochet, and endeavouring to substitute a presbyterian for an episcopal form of ecclesiastical government.

In Scotland, under the leadership of John Knox, they succeeded in establishing an organization on the model of Genevan Calvinism, abolishing the Apostolic Succession and the Book of Common Prayer, and laid waste the churches and their ornaments with such iconoclastic zeal that on visiting Aberbrothock in later years John Wesley exclaimed, "God deliver us from reforming mobs."

In England though Puritanism grew apace its forces became divided by a schism between Presbyterians and Independents, and the queen effectively threw her weight on the side of the establishment, aided by the Archbishop of Canterbury, Whitgift, who had the intellectual support of Richard Hooker and the practical help of his own successor Bancroft, then Bishop of London, and the High Commission. The religious conviction and enthusiasm of Puritanism, however, were unabated if Hooker had succeeded in undermining to a considerable extent its intellectual basis by disposing of the idea that one form of Church government is prescribed as an immutable pattern by divine revelation. Furthermore, he gave a reasoned statement of the comprehensive policy adopted by Elizabeth and her counsellors as the logical outcome of the English Reformation.

BIBLIOGRAPHY

Birt, H. N., *The Elizabethan Religious Settlement*. London, 1907.

Constant, G., *The Reformation in England*. 2 vols. London, 1934, 1941.

Elliot-Binns, L., *The Reformation in England*. London, 1937.

Fleming, J. R., *History of the Church of Scotland*. Edinburgh, 1933.

Gasquet, F. A., *The Eve of the Reformation*. London, 1919.

Gee, H. *Elizabethan Prayer Book*. London, 1902. *The Elizabethan Clergy and the Religious Settlement*. Oxford, 1898, and Hardy, W. J., *Documents Illustrative of English Church History*. London, 1921.

Gore, C., *The Church and the Ministry*. Ed. by C. H. Turner. London, 1919.

Klein, A. J., *Intolerance in the Reign of Elizabeth*. London, 1917.

Lindsay, T. M., *History of the Reformation*. 2 vols. Edinburgh, 1906.

Marti, O. A., *Economic Causes of the Reformation in England*. London, 1929.

Powicke, F. M., *The Reformation in England*. Oxford, 1941.

Pullan, L., *Religion Since the Reformation*. Oxford, 1924.

Smith, H. Maynard, *Pre-Reformation England*. London, 1938.

Smyth, C. H., *Cranmer and the Reformation Under Edward VI*. Cambridge, 1926.

Whitney, J. P., *The Reformation, 1503–1648*. London, 1907.

CHAPTER V

THE NATIONAL CHURCH

THE establishment of a new dynasty with the accession of James I in 1603 destroyed the hopes of those who wished for a radical change in the Elizabethan Settlement. The break with Rome was now absolute and final, and accepted as such by all but the recusant minority, and even among them a quarrel between the Jesuits and the seculars had produced a schism. The Puritans, on the other hand, might well feel that a Scottish king would favour their cause if they were unaware of his profound contempt for and distrust of Presbyterianism, which for him and his successors was thought "to agree as well with a monarchy as God and the devil." "No bishop no king" was the dictum of the Stuarts, who being uncompromisingly convinced of the divine sanction of their own sovereign power, bound the episcopate to themselves as securely as the medieval hierarchy had been bound to the universal papal monarchy by divine decree. Thus, what was virtually a form of national "papalism" arose in England in the seventeenth century with *Ecclesia Anglicana* grounded in a divine right of bishops united with the monarchy in much the same relationship as their predecessors had been with the Pope. This was to have disastrous effects as the century progressed, but it consolidated the Elizabethan Settlement at the beginning of the new dynasty.

THE JACOBEAN CHURCH

Thus, at the conference which assembled at Hampton Court in 1604 to consider the grievances alleged by the Puritans in a petition presented to the king on his way from Scotland into England the previous year, he declared. "I will have one doctrine, one discipline, one religion in substance and ceremony; never speak more to that point, how far you are bound to obey." To the English Reformation Settlement the entire nation must conform or be "harried out of the land—or else worse." With a few minor alterations the Prayer Book was re-issued and the catechism made more explicit in the teaching concerning the sacraments. At the head of Church and State was the throne, regarded as the seat of supreme authority by divine right as the unifying centre of the nation, alike in its spiritual and temporal aspects, so that the one stood or fell with the other. The bishop by virtue of his apostolic origin and royal relationship became quite distinct from the other orders as of the very *esse* of the Church; the distinction between the episcopate and the priesthood, according to Lancelot Andrewes, being *de jure divino*. Therefore, a congregation without bishops, organized that is to say on the Genevan or Presbyterian pattern, was no Church at all and had cut itself off at the same time from the Crown. These Jacobean presuppositions go far to explain the new theological position that was taking shape in England in the seventeenth century, with a central body of what may now be called *Anglicans*, flanked by minorities of Roman Catholics, on the one side, and Puritans, on the other, bound to an establishment to which they found it increasingly impossible to conform. But the facts of the situation had not yet been appreciated by Church or King.

The Intransigent Establishment

If this distinct and uncompromising Anglican theology, firmly based on Scripture and ancient tradition, was the logical outcome of the Elizabethan Settlement, it could not possibly hope to embrace in one visible and organized communion the entire nation now so sharply divided on matters of principle, conviction and tradition. Had James had eyes to see and ears to hear, he would have realized the patent opposition to his policy at the assembly of his first Parliament in 1604, where Puritanism was strongly entrenched. Undeterred by these signs of opposition, Convocation met and drew up a set of 141 canons which have remained in force ever since, except where they have been modified by subsequent legislation.[1] Their

---

[1] A revised set of canons is now in process of promulgation and has been submitted to Convocation for its consideration.

original purpose, however, was mainly to force conformity on the Puritans in such matters as the use of the cope and the surplice, the sign of the cross in baptism and the other controversial injunctions in Parker's Advertisement of 1566, including subscription to the Royal Supremacy, the Articles of Religion and the Book of Common Prayer. This action led to the ejection of some 300 Puritans from benefices, thereby driving them into the position of "dissenters" or "nonconformists." It was not, of course, unreasonable, or indeed unjustifiable, that men who did not and on conscientious grounds could not, believe, teach and maintain the faith and practice of the official Church should be debarred from holding office therein. Their genuine grievance lay in their not being permitted to establish conventicles of their own in which they might worship and carry on their ministerial functions in accordance with their convictions. The time, however, was not yet ripe for an enlightened policy of toleration along these lines. Be they Nonconformists, Papists or Puritans they must be comprehended within and made to conform to the royal episcopal Establishment, or suffer the consequences. And it is to their credit that a considerable proportion chose to suffer rather than to acquiesce in demands which were an affront to their consciences and their rights as free men.

Unfortunately, however, persecution bred plots which only increased the tension between the king and Parliament, and the Church and State. At his opening speech when the houses met, James expressed regret that two bodies existed which refused to live within the fold of the Church of England, and denounced the Puritans for "being discontented with the present government and impatient to suffer any superiority, which maketh their sect unable to be suffered in any well-governed commonwealth." Turning to the Roman Catholics, to whom he was more tolerant, while he recognized that they represented the mother Church, he thought they were defiled by some infirmities and corruptions, and he could not tolerate their priests within his kingdom so long as they upheld the papal claim to dethrone princes and assassinate heretical rulers. The Gunpowder Plot made any reunion with Rome impossible, and deepened the national hatred of the

Papists, with the consequential tightening up of the penal code against them. The Puritans having the support of Parliament awaited the moment in the next reign, when Charles I had ruled on his own initiative for eleven years (1629–40), before resorting to revolutionary measures to overthrow the monarchy.

In the meantime the Roman Catholics were excluded from any office in the State, priests went in daily peril of their lives, and the laity were required to attend Anglican worship in their parish churches on pain of payment of a fine for non-observance. Puritans were similarly proscribed, and their efforts to introduce Sabbatarian legislation involving the suppression of Sunday games and dancing were frustrated. By the time that Charles I came to the throne in 1625, a reaction against Puritan Calvinism had begun to appear, and if the king had combined statesmanship with his strong churchmanship and refined and cultivated tastes, he might have been able to lead the nation into the paths of peace. Already Lancelot Andrewes (1555–1626) by his sound theology, deep piety and saintly life, coupled with his sweet reasonableness and persuasive methods, had vindicated the Anglican position along the lines laid down by Hooker and Jewel against Roman Catholic accretions and Protestant heresies. If he rather than Abbot had been appointed to the Archbishop of Canterbury at the death of Bancroft, the situation might have been saved. Abbot (1562–1633) was a thorough-going Calvinist, ungracious in manner and quite unable to understand the point of view of his opponents, very much as his successor William Laud (1573–1645) repelled even the well-disposed by his abrupt, ostentatious and overbearing behaviour.

LAUD AND "ARMINIANISM"

Laud, however, stood definitely in the Anglican tradition of Hooker and Andrewes, and since this orthodox school was opposed to Puritan Calvinism, it came to be associated in the popular mind with the followers of a Dutch Reformer, Arminius (1560–1609), who effectively attacked the doctrine of predestination and divine grace as taught at Geneva. The Puritans being predominantly Calvinists, placed "Arminian" teaching concerning human freedom and good works on the same level as "Romanism," and in the seventeenth century the designation "Arminian" became a term of abuse comparable to "Popery."[1] Its application to Anglicanism in point of fact was quite unjustified as the only common feature that the Laudian movement in England had with the followers of Arminius in Holland was a rejection of the Calvinistic doctrine of grace. But whereas Arminianism arose as a Dutch reaction against Calvinism, Anglican theology in the seventeenth century was essentially an appeal to the teaching of the Fathers of the Primitive Church as against the ultramontane claims of the Papacy, medieval accretions and foreign Protestantism in its various forms and phases, independent of any one particular school such as Calvinism. For the Jacobean and Caroline divines the English Church was at once Catholic, Reformed and National. While repudiating the papal jurisdiction, it had retained its continuity with the past through the Apostolic Succession of its episcopal ministry, and although it was not very clearly understood exactly what this involved in relation to the validity of the sacraments of non-episcopal bodies, it at least afforded a vital link with the primitive and apostolic church. Jeremy Taylor (1613–67) summed up the situation when he said that though the ordination of Reformed Churches without bishops could not be justified, he was not prepared to determine how far "a good life and a Catholic belief may lead a man in the way to heaven, although the forms of external communion be not observed."

In practice, however, the Church of England in the seventeenth century while it permitted some latitude in isolated instances, as in the case of one De Laune who having received Presbyterian ordination at Leyden was admitted to a benefice by the Bishop of Norwich (Overall) in 1618, as a general rule insisted on episcopal ordination for all its clergy as a *sine quâ non*. Ministers of the French Huguenot communities established in England in the previous reign as an independent body, occasionally were allowed to hold benefices,

---

[1] Thus, the remarkable semi-conventual household of Nicholas Ferrar at Little Gidding in Huntingdonshire was contemptuously described by Puritans as "the Arminian Nunnery."

but this was only a gesture of friendship towards a persecuted minority taking refuge in this country. In fact some pressure was put upon them to induce them to regularize their position by receiving Anglican Orders. In Scotland the situation was very different. There episcopacy was in a fluid condition and all attempts to enforce it failed, notwithstanding the strenuous efforts of Laud to bring the Church north of the Border into line with the Anglican tradition.

The three titular bishops, Spottiswood of Glasgow, Hamilton of Galloway, and Lamb of Brechin, had been consecrated *per saltum* (i.e., they were consecrated to the episcopate without having been previously ordained deacons and priests) by the Bishops of London, Rochester, Ely, and Worcester. Apart from this irregularity their whole position was anomalous and completely out of touch with the life and thought of the country which was predominantly Presbyterian. Thus, it only remained for James I on his own authority to issue canons on the Hooker–Andrewes model, which included the use of a Scottish equivalent of the English liturgy, to produce open rebellion. The project had to be abandoned, and the ill-considered enterprise had disastrous consequences in England where Laud's attempts to establish uniformity and the decencies of worship met with strenuous opposition, partly because he lacked the qualities of statesmanship to deal with the situation, but also because Papists and Puritans were wholly estranged from the Establishment.

It is doubtful, however, whether anyone could have prevented a conflict at this juncture. The throne was vacillating and tottering, Parliament was bent on the destruction of the existing order in Church and State, and social changes were approaching their climax and altering the whole structure of society. The position Elizabeth had tried to stabilize had begun to disintegrate. As a substitute for the papal monarchy the Stuart theory of divine kingship was too secular and nationalistic, fallible and mundane—an outworn survival, in fact, of the royal supernatural sovereignty of the Ancient East (cf. Egypt)—to be a unifying dynamic like the medieval Papacy. Once the king and Parliament came to blows the edifice so laboriously built up by great Englishmen of the calibre of Parker, Hooker, Bancroft and Andrewes, was shattered, though actually not beyond repair. Rome and Geneva had now become serious rivals to Canterbury, and all was ready for a battle royal in which the perennial struggle between the island and the Continent was to be fought out once more, this time under the guise of the factions represented as Cavaliers and Roundheads, or Royalists and Puritans.

The internal situation was complicated by the new elements that had become incorporated in the national religious consciousness. The former solidarity had been completely destroyed by the course of events since the schism with the Holy See in 1533. Christianity in England in the first half of the seventeenth century consisted on the one hand, of a strong and increasing minority of staunch adherents to the papal jurisdiction, known as recusants, undaunted by the serious disabilities and proscriptions they endured as the price they had to pay for the spiritual satisfaction and security they derived from their membership in an infallible and undivided church which knew precisely where it stood and what it taught and demanded of its members. On the other hand stood the Puritans less consolidated but equally opposed in faith and practice to the Anglican Establishment, which seemed to them to be as fundamentally Catholic as for the Papists it was essentially Protestant. To comprehend within one communion powerful groups in the nation so diametrically opposed both in principle and in practice to each other and to the central organization, was to attempt the impossible. Sooner or later the break must come, and the heavier the pressure the greater the tension. The policy of Laud merely hastened the split.

The Cromwellian Interlude

In 1640 the fundamental issue arose over the question of episcopacy, and the bishops did not help their cause by their ostentatious splendour, their enjoyment of high public offices and monopoly of the royal confidence. Their growing unpopularity and the widespread hatred and fear of "popery" made them an easy prey for Puritan propagandists. The attempt to introduce decency of external worship was denounced as an affront to the Reformation so that, as Laud complained, " 'tis superstition nowadays for any man to come with more reverence into a church, than a tinker and his bitch come into an ale-house." The issue, however, went deeper than the ceremonial controversy. Nothing less than the abolition of the apostolic succession would now satisfy the Puritan demands, and this Charles I resolutely refused to consider, knowing full well that therein lay the *esse* of the Anglican position. Consequently, when he was compelled to call Parliament in 1641 the Commons took the matter into their own hands, excluded the bishops from the House of Lords and ordered their impeachment and arrest. The raising of an army, ostensibly to quell an Irish rebellion for which Roman Catholic priests were alleged to have been mainly responsible, was interpreted by the Episcopalian party as a call to arms to defend the king and the Church against Parliamentarian Puritan forces. With the support of the bishops Charles impeached five members of the House of Commons, while the bishops declared that all that was done in the Lords during their absence was null and void. This alienated the sympathies of the temporal peers and further divided the ranks into two hostile groups. Cromwell, a member of the section of Puritans known as Independents, replied by placing himself at the head of his Parliamentary army of Roundheads in defence of the Grand Remonstrance as the Magna Carta of Puritanism.

To obtain the help of Scottish troops, Cromwell was compelled to accept the Presbyterian system as set forth in the Solemn League and Covenant. This brought episcopacy to an end for the time being when the Parliamentarians gained the ascendance in 1645. Churches were sacked, altars destroyed, prayer books burned, the Anglican clergy ejected from all the richer benefices and in their places men appointed by the presbyteries were installed. A Directory of Public Worship was drawn up by the Westminster Assembly "after the pattern of the best reformed churches," and Presbyterian discipline enforced by an ordinance in the Long Parliament in 1646. If this system was never effectively established except in London and the Manchester area, partly because the supply of Puritan ministers and their sympathizers was inadequate to fill the poorer and less important livings, officially the traditional faith and worship of the Church was suspended for fifteen years.

On 10th January, 1645, Laud had paid the supreme penalty of the failure of his policy, and four years later the king followed him to the scaffold. But however faulty may have been their rule and inevitable the consequences of their mistakes, so far as their own fate was concerned, by their deaths they accomplished what they failed to achieve during their lifetimes. As the mystic centre of a Royalist cultus "King Charles the Martyr"[1] became the rallying point for the restoration of the monarchy in the attractive personality of "the king over-the-water," while the Laudian Movement was destined to come into its own after the Restoration settlement of the nation. The Prayer Book continued in use in many obscure parishes, sometimes recited by heart to comply with the law forbidding prayers to be read from a book at public worship. The principles of the Westminster Assembly were foreign to the English tradition, and internecine quarrels between the various Puritan parties—Brownists, or Independents, Separatists, Anabaptists, Levellers and Presbyterians—penal laws against "popery" and "prelacy," the rigid Sabbatarianism, and deprivation of the episcopal clergy, collectively produced a situation which only required the rise of serious constitutional and financial difficulties to produce a strong reaction in favour of the restoration of the monarchy and the National Church.

The death of Cromwell in 1659, followed by a year of anarchy under his son Richard, brought the régime to an end. Its austerity and inquisitorial morality were repugnant, as was the loss of civil liberty, but, nevertheless, the short interlude left an indelible mark on the English character. In addition to the respect for and veneration of the Bible it inculcated, it created a zeal for righteousness and ethical integrity; a keen sense of straight dealing and moral rectitude,

[1] The day after the execution of Charles an unsuspected religious side of his character was revealed by one of his chaplains, John Camden, Dean of Bocking, in a work called *Eikon Basilike*. Like the hair shirt of Becket, this stimulated devotion to the royal martyr, and despite all efforts to suppress the book, edition after edition continued to appear, and acted as a leaven in the development of a cultus.

G

that became the crowning glory and some of the most edifying features of our island civilization. That "an Englishman's word is his bond" is one of the many debts owed to the Cromwellian interlude in our history, as, indeed, indirectly is the growth of toleration, since the freedom of conscience granted to all Puritans and Jews—though denied to the rest of the community—was the beginning of a more liberal attitude towards those who held different views in matters of religion in the commonwealth. Charles I, it is true, had shown leniency to Roman Catholics, but it was the Long Parliament that first recognized the principle of sectarianism under governmental control. This was inevitable in view of the fact that Cromwell was an Independent and yet he relied upon Presbyterianism for the support of his army. But it was inherent in the individualism of the Protestant Reformation, which found its natural expression in independent groups of believers, often mutually antagonistic yet welded together in a loose alliance. Moreover, in England the breakdown of the Elizabethan Settlement in 1649 destroyed once and for all the practicability of a National Establishment embracing all sections of opinion in the country.

THE RESTORATION

This was recognized by Charles II when before his return he declared that "liberty unto tender consciences" should be granted to all, and that "no man shall be disquieted or called in question for difference of opinion in matters of religion which do not disturb the peace of the kingdom." Unlike his father, he himself had little enthusiasm for the Anglican position, and persecution was personally distasteful to him. In so far as he had any religious convictions of his own they were those of continental Catholicism. Puritanism was completely foreign to his temperament, but he made a serious effort to comprehend Presbyterians and Episcopalians in a National Church. Thus, while the Act of Uniformity of 1660 reinstated the Anglican clergy in their sees and benefices, a royal commission was appointed, consisting of twelve of the restored bishops to confer with twelve Puritan divines and nine other theologians on each side, to draw up if possible articles of agreement. The Book of Common Prayer was to be examined in the light of the objections alleged against it and any revisions deemed necessary to be made. Unfortunately, however, in the seventeenth century, despite the move in the direction of sectarianism by the Long Parliament, the idea of a single all-embracing "national religion" was too firmly rooted to be replaced by that of genuine independent growths each planted in its own natural soil. The Reformation may have substituted the sense of individual responsibility, and within very carefully prescribed limits, freedom of thought and liberty of conscience. But it maintained as emphatically as the Holy See the right and duty of suppressing dissent from its rigidly upheld tenets once these had been established, be they Calvinistic, Lutheran, Anglican or what not. Thus, at the Conference called at the Savoy in 1661, the Puritan divines insisted on a complete surrender of the Anglican position both as regards the externals of worship (e.g., kneeling at the reception of Communion, the sign of the cross at baptism, the observance of Lent and Holy Days, and the requirements of the ornaments rubric), and in the teaching of the faith respecting such matters as baptismal regeneration, confirmation, the sacrament of penance and the threefold apostolic ministry. The bishops were equally un-accommodating in their rejection *in toto* of these demands despite the suggestion of Baxter, the Puritan leader, that an alternative liturgy embodying the features insisted upon by his party should be permitted without disturbing the old order.

The Laudian Revival

The political tide was flowing too strongly against compromise with the Cromwellian innovations for the king's policy of toleration and comprehension to be adopted. Parliament was adamant in the rejection of concessions to Puritanism, or of any idea of alternative uses. Therefore, the Conference ended without any attempt to find a realistic solution of the problem, and as uniformity was insisted upon the struggle continued. All holders of ecclesiastical offices were required to be episcopally ordained within two years, and the use of the Prayer Book was enjoined as the sole legal and legitimate form of divine service with a few minor alterations to make the rubrics in the liturgy more explicit, and to emphasize the distinction between the orders of bishop and priest. New occasional prayers were added together with the five prayers at the end of the Jacobean litany. The benediction of the water in the baptismal office was restored and an Order of Baptism of Adults was provided. These changes were justified in a new preface written by Robert Sanderson, Bishop of Lincoln, in which the wisdom of the Church of England was extolled in keeping "a mean between the two extremes," and making only such alterations in the earlier revisions as "tended to the preservation of peace and unity in the Church, and exciting of piety and devotion in the public worship of God."

In this form it was accepted by Convocation and Parliament in 1662, and has ever since remained the official English Prayer Book. All subsequent revisions within the Anglican Communion (i.e., those of the Episcopal Church of Scotland, the United States of America and South Africa) have been based on this model. But for the Puritan party and the Presbyterian it was anathema as it was for the Papists. Therefore, its enforcement by the new Act of Uniformity of 1660 to take effect from St. Bartholomew's Day, 1662, when all ministers who in the meantime had not been episcopally ordained were to vacate their benefices, led to protests with "all the passion imaginable."

The Puritans complained that the promises made by Charles II at Breda before the Restoration had not been fulfilled, but the king was powerless to override Parliament and in an age when dissent was looked upon as a political danger the policy adopted during the Commonwealth had become a boomerang which returned on the heads of those who, as the Speaker in the House of Commons maintained, had been responsible for "trampling upon the discipline and government of the Church." Having outlawed the "prelatists" and "papists" when they were in power themselves, they could hardly expect to escape reciprocal action when they were deposed by the nation in favour of their oppressed rivals. Thus, now that Parliament was as uncompromisingly Anglican as its predecessor had been rigidly Puritan, it lost no time in

passing a series of Acts excluding from membership of cor-
porations all who were not communicants of the National
Church, forbidding "nonconformists" to assemble for worship
over and above five in number, or their preachers to come
within five miles of a town where they had formerly worked,
unless they had taken an oath against the use of arms. It
should be borne in mind, however, that these repressive
measures were directed mainly against the fear of political
risings and a repetition of the recent call to arms by Cromwell
and his followers, though the sacramental test was in fact a
gross abuse of a sacred ordinance. Only men of real cha racter
and conviction would be likely to refuse to "qualify," the
rest, like the Vicar of Bray, would acquiesce, regardless of their
beliefs and spiritual condition.

Moreover, the situation was aggravated by the growing
fear of the king's intention to re-establish the papal jurisdiction.
Thus, when in 1671, he introduced a Declaration of Indulgence
permitting dissenters the right to worship in accordance with
his original undertaking at Breda, even the Puritans themselves
opposed it on the ground that it carried with it the removal
of restrictions placed upon Roman Catholics. To tighten up
the position, in addition to the sacramental requirement, a
declaration against transubstantiation on the part of all holders
of military or civil appointments was added the following
year by the promulgation of the Test Act. But while the
country was determined to resist every effort to restore the
authority of the Apostolic See in England, it was sufficiently
loyal to the monarchy to refuse the attempt made to exclude
the king's brother, James, from the throne, notwithstanding
the fact that he was a Roman Catholic. It was not until he
abused the trust placed in him that he would maintain the
Restoration Settlement in matters of religion, whatever his
own faith and practice might be, that steps were taken to deal
with the situation. The return of the religious orders and the
opening of Roman Catholic chapels were the occasion of
serious riots, and the attempt to instal a Papist as President
of Magdalen College, Oxford, met with strenuous and successful
opposition from the Fellows. The climax was reached in 1688
when the Primate, Sancroft, and six other bishops, refused

to publish in the churches of their dioceses a royal Declaration of Indulgence on the ground that "such a dispensing power may at pleasure set aside all laws ecclesiastical and civil." The challenge to the Anglican tradition and the overt intention to restore the papal jurisdiction was accepted by the entire nation. Amid general rejoicing a verdict of "Not Guilty" was passed on the bishops when they were committed to the Tower by the king, and their acquittal, which carried with it as an inevitable consequence the abdication of James II, was hailed as a national triumph.

THE NON-JURORS AND THE REVOLUTION SETTLEMENT

The arrival of William, Prince of Orange, however, created an impasse for the Church. The Dutch invader was a Calvinist and his claims rested on the sovereignty of Parliament to declare the throne vacant and absolve the bishops and clergy from their oath of allegiance to James II. This raised a critical constitutional and theological issue. Nine of the bishops, including the Primate (Sancroft) and 400 priests, together with practically the whole of the Scottish episcopate and clergy, could not bring themselves to acquiesce in this unprecedented position. Being men of high principle, an argument of expediency carried no conviction with them. Already five of them had preferred to go to the Tower rather than become party to what they believed to be an illegal royal command. Now they were equally ready to accept the ignominious status of Non-jurors for conscience sake and in defence of the liberties of the Church. In so doing, however, they withdrew at a time when their presence and influence were most needed, and produced a schism which continued long after the original dispute had lost its significance and justification. It was such men as Bishop Ken, John Kettlewell, William Law and George Hicks, who might have saved the National Church from becoming merely a department of the State, deriving its authority from Parliament.

Under the Stuarts and the Tudors royal supremacy took the place of papal sovereignty, but the spiritual and temporal spheres remained intact as two integral parts of the one community. The Revolution Settlement of 1689 introduced a new

relationship between Church and State although the attempt
to change the whole character and structure of the establishment by the arbitrary imposition of a new Prayer Book under
the guise of a Comprehension Bill completely failed. Nevertheless, with a Calvinistic monarch the disabilities of the
Puritans and their allies clearly could not be maintained, and
the only way out of the difficulty was to grant religious
liberties to minorities. This was done by the passing of the
Toleration Act of 1689 giving to all except Roman Catholics,
Unitarians and Jews freedom to set up conventicles with
their own ministers but without removing civil disabilities
from nonconformists. Thus, at long last the principle of one
all-embracing National Church was abandoned in favour of
a central Establishment occupying a middle course between
two rival continental systems, Roman and Genevan, one of
which was given official recognition. Clearly it was only a
matter of time before the freedom of worship accorded to
Independents, Presbyterians, Baptists and Quakers, must be
granted to all sorts and conditions of "dissenters," without
discrimination. But in such matters the English mind moves
slowly but none the less surely to its appointed goal.

This new situation raised again the question of the status
in Christendom of the National Church. After a lively discussion it was agreed that it should be officially described as
"Protestant," a term which in the seventeenth century had a
very different meaning from that which it has acquired in the
intervening period. Originally, as we have seen, on the
Continent it was applied exclusively to the Lutherans as
opposed to the Calvinists. By Charles I and Laud it was used
as the equivalent of "Anglican" so that Laud declared on the
scaffold that "he had lived in the Protestant Church of
England," there disclaiming alike allegiance to Roman
Catholicism and Puritanism. To prevent James II interpreting
the phrase "Church of England as by law established" to mean
"the Church of Rome" or "the Church in union with Rome,"
the words "Protestant" and "Reformed" were added to the
official description of the National Establishment; and is still
retained in this sense in the Coronation Rite, to make the
constitutional position quite clear in relation to the Holy See.

But when the Calvinistically minded bishops appointed by WilliamIII on his accession proposed that the Church of England should be described as "a Protestant Church," the Lower House of Convocation, while emphasizing the reformed character of the National Establishment, was careful to draw a distinction between it and the non-episcopal Protestant bodies—Calvinists, Lutherans, Anabaptists, Socinians and Quakers. "Protestant" it might be in respect of Rome, but in relation to the rest of Christendom, it was Catholic and Reformed.

The Scottish Church

In Scotland, on the other hand, the accession of William of Orange brought back Presbyterianism as the official religion and drove the Episcopal Church into the wilderness. The Anglican reaction to the restoration was not very deeply felt. The bishops were nominees of the king and tended to be regarded as political agents rather than successors of the Apostles.

The Knoxian concentric system of Church courts underwent practically no change, and even the English ordinal was not always used at ordinations, while induction to a benefice included the giving of a Bible and the Presbyterian *Book of Discipline* when the keys of the church were received by the new incumbent. The training of the ministry was in the hands of convinced Calvinists, and when the men were admitted to their office, the functions they exercised differed little if at all from those of ordinary Presbyterian ministers. Therefore, Episcopalianism was a fiction except in certain centres, such as in districts of Aberdeenshire, and the Western Isles, Ardnamurchan and Glencoe, and in particular parishes in Edinburgh. Between the Forth and the Tay allegiance was divided with Presbyterianism in the ascendant. Beyond the Tay the sparsely populated north was nearly as solidly Episcopalian (with pockets of Roman Catholicism near the Caledonian Canal, in Braemar and on the Western Islands) as the south-west was Presbyterian. But notwithstanding the prevailing Calvinistic tendency throughout the greater part of the country, a latent Jacobean and non-juring movement made Episcopalianism suspect of subversive political intentions.

This encouraged ruthless suppression, deprivation and per-secution, until at length, in the next century, a veritable reign of terror ensued.

LATITUDINARIANISM

In England efforts were directed mainly against Roman Catholics, but the Revolution of 1689 marked the beginning of the decline of the Laudian Movement and the ascent of a new school composed of "men of latitude," strongly Whig in their politics, Erastian in their churchmanship and rationalistic in their intellectual outlook. The successors of devout and devoted parish priests like George Herbert of Bemerton and the Ferrars at Little Gidding had become Non-jurors by the beginning of the eighteenth century,[1] and the new Archbishop of Canterbury, Tillotson, had been ejected from his chair at Cambridge in 1660 as a Presbyterian. Although after the Savoy Conference he conformed and was ordained, he had no conception of the Anglican position and its tradition. This might be said of many of the bishops of the eighteenth century. They were men of learning and breadth of view, strongly influenced by the new scientific and philosophic spirit that had replaced the narrow theological outlook of post-Reformation controversy. But they were not calculated to arouse religious enthusiasm in an apathetic age.

The old finality in thought as well as in belief had gone under the influence of the new empiricism of Descartes, Locke and Hume. The solid fabric of the universe had passed into a kaleidoscopic unreality of change, and reason appeared to have lost its former validity. To doubt the existence of everything except one's own ideas is to sow the seeds of complete scepticism which must end in loss of faith and eventually in loss of nerve. Thus, Locke having denied the objective reality of secondary qualities and Bishop Berkeley, in his idealistic defence of theism and Christianity, going a step further denying the reality of primary qualities, it only remained for Hume

[1]Thus, Ken (1637-1711) when he was Vicar of Little Easton, in Essex, said Morning and Evening Prayer daily in his parish church, and Lady Maynard had the offices read to her in her house when she was unable to go to the daily services.

to reduce everything to a flux of events with no adequate ground for believing in mind itself. The wheel having gone full circle, absolute scepticism became the prevailing influence in what is known as the period of Enlightenment.

In the domain of religion Catholicism had lost its solidarity, Protestantism had broken up into sectarianism, and in England Puritanism and Caroline Anglicanism were spent forces. All this had a damping effect upon enthusiasm and fostered a general atmosphere of doubt, uncertainty and absence of zeal. Free thought became the minor premiss in an argument wherein natural rights were the major premiss and natural religion was the conclusion. This found expression in the Deistic movement as an attempt to get behind the theology of revealed religion to the belief in a beneficent Creator as a remote First Cause far removed from the actual world and the immediate life of men. But since the idea of an overruling Providence ordering all things for the best was retained, this gave Joseph Butler (1692–1752), Bishop of Durham, an opportunity to demonstrate in his famous *Analogy of Religion* (1738) that, granting the authority of human reason, the objections brought against the God of revelation could be turned with equal force against the God of nature. Basing his argument on the eighteenth century notion of probability as the guide of life in a world of uncertainties, he built up the case for Christianity by the inductive method, in keeping with the spirit of the age, but transcending it as a contribution to thought of abiding value and a model of precise and reasoned apologetic.

THE NATIONAL CHURCH IN THE EIGHTEENTH CENTURY

The National Church, therefore, was not without its effective champions in men like George Berkeley, Joseph Butler and Edmund Gibson, at a time when, as Butler recognized, "the general decay of religion in this nation" was only too apparent. The Church in England unquestionably had struck a bald patch. But if there was little interest in, understanding of, or zeal for the Anglican position, as had been displayed by the Caroline divines in the previous period, and as was revealed by their successors in the reign of Queen Anne

(which witnessed a remarkable if sporadic outburst of enthusiasm finding expression in the creation of numerous church
societies and the building of parish churches of surpassing
beauty[1]), the practice of religion was still maintained. Thus,
as Dr. Lowther Clarke has shown, the publications of the
Society for the Promotion of Christian Knowledge (founded
in 1698, and supplemented in 1701 by the Society for the
Propagation of the Gospel) reveal that a genuine piety still
survived. The Eucharist was all too infrequently celebrated,
except among the Non-jurors, though weekly Celebrations were
not uncommon in London and other large towns, but efforts
were made to inculcate a devotional approach to the altar by
the production of manuals to help communicants in their
personal preparation for Communion, and to provide a guide
to the liturgy. At St. Bartholomew's, Smithfield, in 1748 the
communicants numbered as many as a thousand on an ordinary
Sunday, and at St. James's, Piccadilly, "multitudes" are said
to have "crowded up to the altar without superstition or
tumult" every month. At St. Thomas's, Soho, there was
Communion every first and third Sunday of the month and
on great festivals, as was also the case at St. Dunstan's, Stepney,
and many other London churches, while at St. Mary-le-Bow
Celebrations followed Morning Prayer on all holy days.
Similarly in Oxford there was a weekly Eucharist at Christ
Church. So sacramental life was by no means dead in the
post-Revolution period.

The weakness of the National Church lay in its narrow
Erastianism and isolation. Its essential Anglican structure was
preserved and faithful witness was borne by churchmen of all
schools of thought. Indeed, an age that produced William Law
and enabled him to exercise a powerful influence on his own
day and generation cannot have been wholly spiritually mori-
bund. But the doubt, uncertainty and scepticism manifest on
all sides had a blighting effect on religious enthusiasm. That
Hoadly (1676-1761), the non-resident Bishop of Bangor,
should have denied the very existence of the Church as a

---

[1] Sir Christopher Wren (1632-1723) was responsible for the erection
of no less than fifty-three parish churches in London alone in addition to
St. Paul's Cathedral.

spiritual society is perhaps hardly surprising in view of the new relation that existed between the National Establishment and Parliament. The suppression of Convocation from 1717 to 1853 prevented the bishops from exercising corporate action by constitutional means, and only in the House of Lords could they control legislation as a body, and then as nominees of a political party. Under such circumstances Erastianism was bound to flourish and lethargy born of frustration settled as a blight upon the religious life of the nation until it was dispelled in the middle and latter part of the century by the rise of a new Evangelical movement which the National Church was incapable of understanding or bringing under its directive control before it had formed a rival schismatic organization. It is indeed one of the major tragedies of the period that a great spiritual force through lack of sympathetic guidance was allowed to drift into dissent.

BIBLIOGRAPHY

Abbey, C. J., and Overton, J. H., *The English Church in the Eighteenth Century.* 2 vols. London, 1878.

Abbey, C. J., *The English Church and its Bishops,* 1700–1800. London, 1887.

Acton, Lord, *History of Freedom and other Essays.* London, 1907.

Ady, C. M., "Post-Reformation Episcopate" in *The Apostolic Ministry.* Ed. K. E. Kirk. London, 1946.

Clarke, W. K. Lowther, *Eighteenth Century Piety.* London, 1944.

Duncan-Jones, A. S., *Archbishop Laud.* London, 1927.

Figgis, J. N., *The Divine Right of Kings.* 2nd Ed. London, 1922.

Frere, W. H., *The English Church in Reigns of Elizabeth and James.* London, 1904.

Gee, H., and Hardy, W. J., *Documents Illustrative of English Church History,* 1898.

Henderson, G. D., *Religious Life in Seventeenth-Century Scotland.* Cambridge, 1937.

Hutton, W. H., *William Laud.* London, 1895. *History of the English Church,* 1625–1714. London, 1903.

More, P. E., and Cross, F. L., *Anglicanism.* London, 1935.

Sykes, N., *Church and State in England in the Eighteenth Century.* Cambridge, 1934.

Stephens, W., *History of the Scottish Church*. 2 vols. London, 1893–6.

Trevor-Roper, H. R., *Archbishop Laud*. London, 1940.

Usher, R. G., *The Reconstruction of the English Church*. 2 vols. New York, 1910. *High Commission*. Oxford, 1913.

Wand, J. W. C., *A History of the Modern Church*. London, 1930.

Wickham Legg, J., *English Church Life from the Restoration to the Tractarian Movement*. London, 1914.

CHAPTER VI

NONCONFORMITY
AND THE CHURCHES IN ENGLAND

THE course of events which reached their natural and logical conclusion in the Toleration Act of 1690 when "their majesties' Protestant subjects differing from the Church of England" were granted liberty to establish independent congregations without let or hindrance, marked the end of the Church-nation. Hitherto one religious system alone had been tolerated in the country, be it Papal, Anglican or Puritan, and whatever latitude might be permitted in matters of belief and practice, a minimum of "conformity" was required to the fundamental principles and structure of the established régime. Prior to the Henrician Schism with the Holy See in the sixteenth century, the Church in England was an integral part of Western Christendom, and whatever local uses, customs, rights and privileges were claimed, exercised or allowed from time to time, the unity of the ecclesiastical organization and juris-diction was never in question. Moreover, as we have seen, while the breach with Rome, coinciding with the new reform movement on the Continent, inevitably drove the English Church into the anti-papal camp, it did not materially alter the traditional conception of ecclesiastical unity in the nation. Church and State remained a single entity, or rather two aspects of one complete whole, each subject to the Royal Supremacy, as formerly both had been ultimately under the authority of the Papacy as the final court of appeal. Therefore, sectarianism could not be allowed without the danger of grave injury to the solidarity of the body politic, for in all ages religion has been the consolidating dynamic in society.

In the meantime the traditional doctrine of the Church as the divinely founded visible society, or *ecclesia*, with an ordered ministry, sacramental life, revealed faith, supernatural authority and organic unity of its own, had been abandoned in the majority of reformed communities in favour of the notion of congregations of believers gathered together in the Spirit of Christ as the elect people of God. Thus, for Luther the Church was composed of those who had been chosen by divine love and justified by faith in the redeeming death of Christ. Wherever the Gospel was truly preached and the sacraments administered there was the true Church, the pastors being the expression of the priesthood of all believers. "He who does not preach the Word is in no way a priest; and the sacrament of Orders is nothing else than a ceremony for choosing preachers." Calvin regarded the Church as the body of the elect from among whom pastors and teachers were selected to minister to and instruct the company of believers. Ordination by laying on of hands, he maintained, had apostolic sanction but was not a divine precept. The apostles, prophets and evangelists mentioned in Ephesians iv, 11 "were not instituted in the Church to be perpetual" even though God occasionally raised up apostles, or at least evangelists, in their stead, as in the case of the Reformers. Except in these very special instances it was "the call" given through the voice of the congregation that constituted the essence of the ministry, ordination being the seal placed upon the selection when it had been confirmed by the pastors, and approved by the civil power. Teachers were similarly admitted to their office after the external call and examination by the pastors, but elders were appointed by the civil council. The ministers and elders collectively formed the consistory and exercised spiritual authority over the elect company of believers.

PRESBYTERIANISM

This was the basis of Presbyterianism as it was organized by John Knox (1505-1572) and his followers in Scotland as a system of ecclesiastical government. The conception of the parity of ministers became an essential feature of the true Church as the scheme took shape under the influence of Andrew Melville (1545-1622). The merging of bishop and presbyter in one order eliminated the episcopal office in its traditional form since the reconstituted presbyter consisted of ministers commissioned to teach and administer the sacraments by the election and "call" of the congregations which they were to serve, assisted by lay-elders and deacons.[1] Ministers and ruling elders of individual congregations assembled together as a Kirk-Session, or lowest form of Church court, to administer local parochial affairs. At a very early period Presbyteries were formed consisting of all the teaching ministers and ruling elders for each session in a district, presided over by a moderator, who regulated the business but did not exercise any special ministerial or judicial authority comparable to that of a bishop. The oversight of congregations and all legislative, executive and judicial functions were vested in the Presbytery as a whole, subject to the control of the Synod, or Provincial Court (representing the sum of its Presbyteries since it was composed of ministers and elders from each of the congregations in the area), and the General Assembly as the supreme authority, or National Synod, embracing all the Synods within the Nation.

It is in this carefully devised scheme that the fundamental unity of the Presbyterian system has been maintained and its theory of the ministry given expression. Thus, the Presbytery has become the substitute for episcopal jurisdiction, ordination and diocesan organization. It sustains the call of the prophetic minister, examines his fitness and ordains and inducts him to his pastorate. It may exercise a similar function in relation to the ruling elders unless in particular cases this is done by the Kirk-Session. The Presbytery has oversight of all the churches in its district together with the superintendence of the lesser courts, just as it is responsible for the maintenance of discipline, the training of ordinands and the election of representatives to the Synod and General Assembly, wherein lies the plenitude of power subject to the constitution of the Church and the rights of the constituent bodies.

This elaborate organization never made the same progress in England as it did in Scotland, despite the influence of Thomas Cartwright, the Elizabethan Lady Margaret Professor of Divinity at Cambridge, who was an ardent supporter of the Calvinistic Movement. Presbyterianism was not adapted

---

[1]Deacons, being merely secular officials, have tended to drop out of the system.

to the conditions under which a proscribed Nonconformity had to function, and when Cromwell gained the ascendance and had to establish the Solemn League and Covenant between 1643 and 1648, the interlude proved to be as temporary as it was unpopular. The Independents were predominant in the army, and the subsequent course of events which brought Cromwell to supreme power reacted adversely against Presbyterianism in England so that before the Restoration it had failed to consolidate its position. While Charles II was not unfavourably disposed towards it as a foil to secure toleration for the papal jurisdiction, the Act of Uniformity drove it into the ranks of Nonconformity, and so fostered a closer alliance with Congregationalism between 1660 and 1690. But by tradition and outlook the Englishman was not Genevan, and Presbyterianism never secured an assured position south of the Border. There it tended either to lapse into Unitarianism or to become essentially a Scottish community. In Scotland the State connection produced schisms over the question of patronage and the relation with the civil authority, but since 1900, when the Free Church and the United Presbyterians were amalgamated into the United Free Church of Scotland, considerable progress has been made towards a greater unity, with reciprocal effects in America and other parts of the world.

INDEPENDENCY AND CONGREGATIONALISM

The parallel Puritan movement in England in the sixteenth century, usually associated with the name of Robert Browne, adopted a much simpler system of organization in which each congregation was regarded as an independent church. Attempts to set up private groups of "Separatists" were made in the reign of Elizabeth before Browne formulated a "congregational" theory of government in theological terms. But it was his tractates that laid down fundamental principles which were adopted by Baptists, Plymouth Brethren and Unitarians, as well as by Independents or Congregationalists. Theologically Browne was a Calvinist, and like the continental Protestant Reformers, taking Scripture as his sole guide, he sought to reproduce in its pristine simplicity the apostolic fellowship

H

and worship. This, as he thought, consisted of congregations of believers gathered together in a covenant relationship with God in Christ, on equal terms with each other as kings, priests and prophets. The officers were to be tried and examined by the whole congregation unless a particular man had given proof of his godliness by establishing a church (i.e., a congregation) on his own initiative. Then he had to be received as its guide and teacher (i.e., minister) without any specific ordination by other pastors. But when an already constituted congregation required a new officer the free and clear "consent of the people gathered by the elders or guides" must precede the appointment, just as it was the duty of the congregation to depose an unworthy officer. The authorization of the minister was usually accompanied by "prayer and the imposition of the elders' hands," but this method was not regarded as an essential requirement, as in episcopal ordination. Indeed, it was declared that the laying on of hands should be omitted when "it is turned into pomp or superstition." The holding of synods and councils was to be voluntary rather than an integral part of church government. Each congregation must be a completely independent entity, in the same way as the ministry is merely a particular form of the "priesthood of the laity," if indeed the terms "clerical" and "lay" are distinguishable in this system.

As "Brownism" or "Separatism" developed into Congregationalism or Independency as an ecclesiastical polity destined to play an important part in the religious and political life of the nation, and, in fact, throughout the Protestant world, it was compelled to formulate a theology in accordance with its system of church government, despite its theoretical repudiation of a credal basis and centralized constitution. On the initial hypothesis that each separate and independent congregation is a self-determining church subject to no external control, anything in the nature of a dogmatic test of orthodoxy in matters of faith for the denomination as a whole was carefully excluded. The minister was chosen and appointed by a particular congregation to preach the Gospel as he understood it in the light of his own spiritual experience; though in fact, in common with Puritanism in general, Calvinism was the theological basis of the movement, and the Westminster Confession was the accepted form of faith with certain modifications. Baptism was retained as the initial sacrament of the Gospel but transformed into a "seal" of a "covenant" relationship with God in Christ, established either as the birthright of children born of believing parents, or, in the case of adults, the confirmation of their church membership rather than, as in Catholic theology, a regenerative initiation into the mystical body of Christ. Similarly, the Lord's Supper was administered as the seal of divine communion along the lines laid down by Calvin.

Public worship followed the normal Genevan form of extempore prayer, the reading of the Scriptures, often with interpretations verse by verse, the singing of psalms and the preaching of a sermon, with the addition of hymns since the beginning of the eighteenth century, and other musical enrichments. The return to liturgical worship which in recent years has become prominent in some non-episcopal denominations, has not made very much progress as yet in congregationalism except in a few isolated instances, of which the recent attempts at the restoration of Catholic forms of service at King's Weigh House, London, by Dr. Orchard, was a notable example. The dislike of fixed forms of prayers, however, is now generally less apparent than formerly, and the imposition of hands by a minister or elder in the appointment of pastors has been adopted as an alternative to the "right hand of fellowship." The late Dr. Garvie estimated that it is now in use in about 70 per cent of Congregational ordinations, thereby giving a rather wider recognition of the office, over and above that of the particular community in which the minister is to exercise his pastoral functions.

This fellowship of the local churches in a larger organization has been expressed in the foundation of county and national Congregational Associations and Unions, and since 1891 an International Council with world-wide representation has met at intervals. To give greater solidarity to the organization regional superintendents or moderators (who need not necessarily be ministers) have been appointed to act in an advisory capacity in concert with the county union and executives on questions of administration. Care has been taken, however, not to infringe upon the autonomy of each independent congregation as the fundamental principle of the entire system. A State connection prominent in Genevan Calvinism for the most part has been repudiated except in America, where in the New England colonies, after the arrival of the Pilgrim Fathers, Congregationalism became an established religion. Thus, in Massachusetts and New Haven the political franchise was limited to members of the denomination during the middle portion of the seventeenth century, and it was not until 1834 that the last link with the civil power was severed in the United States. Any form of "Establishment," however, hardly can have a rightful place in a polity expressly designed to be a free association of self-determining local congregations, each exercising its own government as an independent company of believers in a "willing covenant made with their God" and with one another.

THE BAPTISTS

Allied to the Congregationalists in church government and to the Calvinists in their avowal of personal religious experience in baptism, are the fellowship of believers called Baptists. Where originally they differed from the theology of the continental reformed churches was in the place, manner and function of the sacrament in the profession of the Christian faith. It was generally agreed among the Protestant Reformers that baptism is primarily an assurance of forgiveness and of imputed righteousness as against the Roman and Anglican doctrine that the grace of regeneration is conferred in order to remove the guilt of original sin. But if it is the sign and seal satisfying and confirming God's promises to the believer, as Calvin insisted, rather than an objective sacramental gift of grace, its efficacy would seem to depend on the faith of the recipient, and presupposes penitence and personal surrender to Christ. Consequently, it is reasonable to conclude that the administration of the rite should be confined to those who have passed through this spiritual experience.

This was the logical position maintained by John Smith who became a Separatist in 1605 and emigrated to Holland with some other Independents. In Amsterdam he came under the influence of Anabaptist, or Mennonite, teaching, baptized himself, separated from the Independents, rejected infant baptism as an anomaly, and formed the first Baptist Church. In 1611 the earliest Baptist Confession was printed in Amsterdam in which it was declared that "every church is to receive all their members by baptism upon the confession of their faith and sins, wrought by the preaching of the Gospel according to the primitive institution and practice. And therefore churches constituted after any other manner, or of any other persons, are not according to Christ's testament. That baptism or washing with water is the outward manifestation of dying unto sin and walking in newness of life; and therefore in no wise appertaineth to infants." Smith died in 1612 and the same year his collaborator, Thomas Helwys, returned to England and formed the first Baptist congregation in Newgate Street in London. In 1633 a rival organization of Calvinistic origin was established in Southwark under the name of the Particular Baptist Church.

The earlier "General Baptist" denomination was Arminian in its doctrine of "general redemption" as against the predestinarianism of the Calvinistic Particulars, who were also rigidly "fundamentalist" in their interpretation of the verbal inspiration of Scripture, and exclusive in their membership, maintaining that since the true Church is composed of believers, only those whose public profession of faith has received the seal of baptism can be regarded as belonging to it. The Arminian, or General Baptists, on the other hand, repudiated the Calvinistic doctrine of predestination in favour of individual responsibility and salvation of all men, and adopted a more liberal attitude towards church membership irrespective of baptism. They also did not insist upon marriage within the connection, a rule enforced by the Particulars. Both groups however, were agreed upon the rejection of infant baptism, and eventually they reached a common mind about the substitution of immersion or "dipping" for aspersion or sprinkling in the administration of the baptismal rite. But the mutual abhorrence of creeds led to a great variety of "confessions" setting forth the doctrinal basis of the different schools of thought and practice comprehended within the movement. In the eighteenth century a section of the General Baptists moved in the direction of Unitarianism thereby causing a split in 1770, when the orthodox portion formed itself into a "New Connection," while the Particulars became more rigidly Calvinistic and exclusive. But the distinction between "General" and "Particular" has now largely disappeared within the denomination.

In organization and worship there is similarity in custom among all English-speaking Baptists. Like the Congregationalists, every church is self-governing with its pastors and deacons appointed on a strictly non-sacerdotal basis by its own members, and subject to no external jurisdiction. Public worship follows the "Genevan" or "synagogue" model commonly adopted by English Nonconformists, with extempore prayers, Scripture reading, psalms, hymns and preaching in unconsecrated buildings designed for this type of divine service. An important feature of the denomination is its missionary enterprise which has carried it to most parts of the world. It is indeed claimed that congregations have arisen spontaneously as a result of the distribution of copies of the Bible without any specific teaching or organization on the part of adherents, but this requires further investigation in the light of our present day anthropological knowledge of the diffusion of religious institutions and cultural traits.

THE SOCIETY OF FRIENDS

One of the most remarkable "congregational" movements, wholly nonsacramental in character, was instituted in the seventeenth century by George Fox (1624–91) in an attempt to form a nonsectarian society based on spiritual experience known as the Inward Light. Like the Silesian shoemaker, Jacob Boehme (1575–1624), who in a reaction against all theological and institutional expressions of Christianity urged the re-living of the Christ-life in the conquest of self by the divine spirit in the soul, Fox maintained that "every man was enlightened by the Divine Light of Christ, and I saw it shine through all; and that they that believed in it came out of condemnation and came into the Light of Life, and became children of it. But they that hated it, and did not believe in it, were condemned by it, though they made a profession of Christ. This I saw in the pure opening of the Light without the help of any man, neither did I then know where to find it in the Scriptures, though afterwards, searching the Scriptures, I found it."

But while, like the rest of the Protestant Reformers, Fox sought inspiration in the Bible, his conception of salvation differed fundamentally from the Calvinistic doctrine of election and the "Arminian" (i.e., Lutheran) belief in justification by faith of all men in the finished work of Christ as Redeemer. All theological schemes and theories were as anathema to him, in fact, as were ecclesiastical systems and organizations, Catholic or Protestant. Christianity was a way of life, a mystical experience of the inner self here and now, a waiting upon the Lord in silence and confidence until His Word took possession of the heart, His Voice was heard speaking to the soul and His Spirit animated the entire being. It was in the "sacrament of silence" that Christ was to be sought and found, and the whole of life became "incarnational" in His indwelling Light. "In all things we found the Light which we were enlightened withall, and all mankind (which is Christ) to be alone and onelie sufficient to bring to life and eternal salvation."

A direct, secret and incommunicable knowledge of God received in contemplation and mystical experience has been a recurrent feature of Christianity, taken over from Judaism and Neoplatonism under the influence of St. Augustine, the Pseudo-Dionysius, St. Gregory the Great, and St. Bernard, and incorporated in the institutional religion of the medieval Church. Thus, several of the great theologians of the thirteenth century (e.g., St. Bonaventura, Albertus Magnus and St. Thomas Aquinas) were also mystics, while in the sixteenth century St. Catherine of Genoa and the Discalced Carmelites, St. Teresa of Avila and St. John of the Cross, combined a profound mysticism with dogmatic theology and the practice of institutional religion. It was out of this tradition that Protestant mysticism was born and brought into relation with the new emphasis on the revealed Word in the Scriptures. But severed from its moorings in a visible Church in and through which divine grace is mediated in sacramental ordinances by a divine-human intercourse and relationship, it seemed to render entirely superfluous the aid and intervention of any prescribed form of worship, theology, organization or ministry. The operation of the Spirit, it was maintained, was in no way limited to externalized channels in time, place or person. Therefore, Fox and his followers ceased from "the teachings of all men and their words, and their worships and their temples and all their baptismes and churches," and "met together often and waited upon the Lord in pure silence from our own words and all men's words, and hearkened to the voice of the Lord and felt His Word in our hearts to burn up and beat down all that was contrary to God."

At these informal meetings so great was the emotion that it produced trembling and quaking when they prayed, and thereby caused them to be called "Quakers," a name already applied to other sects which behaved in this manner. But a mystical silence was and has remained the principal feature of their gatherings and the centre of their spiritual life. In quietness and confidence they drew their strength from the invisible presence of the Spirit of God, but while this was equated with the indwelling light of Christ, they refused to commit themselves to any position respecting the inspiration of Scripture, or of the person and work of Christ as the Incarnate Lord and Redeemer of mankind. This brought them into conflict with Puritans and Anglicans alike, especially as they maintained the possibility of attaining complete victory over sin in this life. But notwithstanding these controversies and the persecutions they endured under the legal proscription of Dissenters before the passing of the Toleration Act in 1690, steadfastly refusing to worship in secret their numbers increased until in England they reached their peak of 60,000 at the end of the seventeenth century. Since then, however, the movement has declined, though its influence has been out of all proportion to its numerical strength which is now estimated at 160,000.

Adopting their own manner of speech, form of dress, and behaviour in society, their steadfastness and transparent sincerity gradually won the respect it deserved, and an increasing public recognition of their scruples in such matters as unconditional refusal to take any part in wars, or to swear oaths. Content to be "the peculiar people," cut off from the affairs of their local government and the arts, they devoted themselves to commerce, like the Jains and Parsees in India; their industry and integrity bringing its own reward in phenomenal success. This has enabled them to respond liberally to the calls of philanthropy and education, and among their many good works, adult schools, settlements, homes for the aged, and similar social institutions stand out conspicuously. But despite all these efforts for the betterment of mankind, the Society of Friends has remained a small and exclusive movement spread over a very wide area in Europe and America. Mysticism may be "the raw material of all religion," but unless it finds expression in a rational theology and institutional organization, it tends to substitute an immanental humanism not far removed from a pantheistic absorption in the divine as the "inner light" of every man, for a personal union with God as the sovereign ruler, redeemer and judge of the universe in Whose sustaining and fostering care lies its hope of perfection.

Moreover, the facts of religious experience are not self-evident, or a guarantee of the truth of the meaning read into it by the individual concerned. Thus, the spiritual visions of St. Teresa or St. John of the Cross and the inward light of Master Eckart or George Fox, though interpreted in terms of the Christian thought and practice which formed their respective backgrounds, would have been given a very different evaluation by a Hindu mystic or a Taoist quietist. The data of mystical experience are not pure data. They are conditioned by the system of beliefs they imply, and involve an interpretation in relation to a specific theology. If this is lacking they will not be likely to carry much conviction outside a very small eclectic circle of similarly illuminated souls, and even within this select company there may well be a wide divergence, as for example, between the dogmatic Catholic theology of St. Teresa and the undefined "divine light of Christ" of Fox. Indeed, the Quakers maintained that the principle of the inward light as a direct source of divine knowledge was higher than the testimony of Scripture as well as superior to reason, conscience and all credal formulations of Christianity. Consequently, it is not surprising that a section of the movement, holding lightly to the orthodox doctrine of the person and work of Christ, drifted towards Unitarianism and a vague theism, with little or no distinctively Christian content. In reaction to this latitudinarianism an effort was made to return to the earlier evangelical position, but the permanent contribution of the Society of Friends to English Christianity has been on the side of its moral and social witness rather than in the sphere of specifically religious thought and practice.

UNITARIANISM

A more radical departure from traditional orthodoxy was made in the seventeenth century when John Biddle (1616–62) contended that Trinitarian terminology was unscriptural particularly in relation to the deity of the Holy Spirit. On the Continent an Italian, Faustus Socinus (1539–1604) in Poland had already attacked the evangelical doctrine of salvation and maintained that Christ was human by origin though raised to divine status as the official representative of God. It was not until the next century, however, that the movement (variously described as "Socinian," "Arian," and finally Unitarian) made much progress in England, though it was sufficiently established to be proscribed, with Roman Catholicism, under the Toleration Act of 1689. But it was more a mode of thought than an organized religious sect, and as such became increasingly prevalent in educated circles as rationalism predominated in the eighteenth century. John Locke (1632–1704), for example, the founder of a new empiricism in philosophical thought, in his *Letters on Toleration* (1689–92) and the *Essay on the Human Understanding* (1690) stressed the futility of empty verbiage and an acquiescence in traditional assumptions which take the place of honest intellectual inquiry. Applying these principles to religion, he vindicated man's right to freedom, and argued the absurdity of forcing all men to the acceptance of particular dogmatic beliefs when the theological presuppositions are based on such unsubstantial foundations. Going back to the Gospels he reduced the one essential article of faith to the Messiahship of Christ, and although he regarded the Scriptures as ultimate divine revelations without any mixture of error, the miracles were to be judged by the doctrines and not the doctrines by the miracles—a sound principle but an innovation in those days.

All this, of course, favoured the Unitarian position and the prevailing Deism of the age. Installing themselves in chapels and meeting-houses where doctrinal tests were not enforced, they gained platforms for the dissemination of the movement, though it was not until 1774 that the first Unitarian chapel as such was opened in London—in Essex Street. It was at this time that Joseph Priestley, whose pioneer researches in chemistry gave him a position of distinction, lent powerful support to the cause, and although it was technically pro-scribed,[1] chapels multiplied, so that by the beginning of the nineteenth century they were estimated at over 200. The demand for complete liberty of thought and practice, however, reacted against a corporate denominational life and allegiance with the result that, despite the zeal and distinction of its adherents, who included James Martineau, Francis William Newman, and in America William Channing, Emerson and Longfellow, it was too cold, rationalistic, undefined and negative to become an effective religious force. Like the Quakers its aims have been mainly philanthropic and humanitarian, a cult of reason being the basis of its belief and practice.

METHODISM

At the opposite pole stands the great revival of evangelical enthusiasm in the middle of the eighteenth century with which the name of John Wesley will always be associated. Born of Nonconformist stock, though actually the son of the Rector of Epworth, in Lincolnshire, he and his brother Charles inherited the sturdy and independent qualities of dissent which prevailed in the pious and orthodox home in which they were nurtured. At the age of sixteen John went up to Oxford as a commoner of Christ Church, where he was followed six years later by his brother Charles. John having been elected to a fellowship at Lincoln, they soon gathered round them in Oxford a small group of devout churchmen known as the

[1]The statutes proscribing Unitarianism were not repealed until 1813.

"Holy Club," who communicated every Sunday, fasted on Wednesdays and Fridays until 3 p.m., made their confessions to a priest, visited the sick and the prisoners in Bocardo, the city jail, met together several evenings in the week for the study of the New Testament, and endeavoured to keep themselves unspotted from the world. In short, it was the precepts and ideals of the Non-juring William Law's *Serious Call to a Devout Life* that they tried to adopt; and their methodical way of life, both in study and practice, earned them the title "Methodists," or "Bible-moths."

In 1735 John and Charles set off for America to undertake missionary work in Georgia under the auspices of the Society for the Propagation of the Gospel. During the voyage they came into intimate contact with some members of a highly emotional pietistic German sect known as Moravians, which at the beginning of the century had arisen in Saxony under the influence of Count Nicolaus von Zinzendorf (1700–1760), who transformed his estate into a religious settlement called Herrnhut, "the Watch of the Lord." There the Moravians lived a common life and made the colony a centre of ardent missionary enterprise which carried their enthusiastic pietism to most parts of the world. It was from them that the Wesleys gained a fuller knowledge of the "twice-born" type of conversion that was a characteristic feature of the sect, and to which they both seem to have been temperamentally inclined. Thus, on their return to England in 1738 they underwent a religious experience comparable to that of St. Augustine in the Milanese garden and of Luther on the Santa Scala at Rome. It was, in fact, as he listened to the reading of Luther's preface to the Epistle to the Romans in a meeting house in Aldersgate Street that John Wesley, as he relates, in eager expectation of a spiritual crisis such as his brother had experienced a few days before, felt his heart strangely warmed and realized that he did trust in Christ as his personal Saviour, who had taken away his sins.

From then onwards he regarded himself as a reborn Christian and devoted the rest of his life to proclaiming, in season and out of season, regardless of diocesan organization and all ecclesiastical proprieties, the unsearchable riches of

Christ as a free gift of divine grace. At Bristol, Newcastle-on-Tyne, Kingswood and Moorfields, to mention but a few of his more prominent centres, crowds flocked to hear his simple and fervent evangelical message, preached with all the vigour and sincerity of St. Francis, and having a freshness of appeal in striking contrast to the lethargy of the parish churches and the sectarian controversies and bitterness of Nonconformity. A mass psychology was rapidly created and strange scenes were witnessed at the great gatherings in which the tension was such that hefty colliers and sturdy farm labourers rolled on the ground in a state of hypnotic convulsion. A veritable wave of new birth passed over the industrial districts which at the time were springing up with lightning rapidity in the North and Midlands. It spread through the agricultural country-side in East Anglia and thence to Devon and Cornwall, carry-ing all before it. Labourers, farm hands, miners, artisans and shopkeepers, for whom the philosophy of Locke, Butler and Berkeley, the quietism of Fox and the stern Calvinism of the Puritan sects had little or no attraction, were saved from spiritual ruin by the new "Arminian" revival.

That the Church of England lacked the vision and wisdom to utilize the crusade will always remain an outstanding example in history of lost opportunities. Unlike the other reforming movements, the Wesley revival began within the National Church with no wish or intention of separating from it. The initiators were priests in Anglican Orders, and at first there was no radical departure in doctrine or practice from the faith of the Establishment, though this can hardly be extended to the sphere of order. Free-lances as they were it was only with reluctance and through pressure of events, that the original Wesleyans were driven to set up an inde-pendent sectarian organization. Trained in the Laudian tradition, the brothers Wesley were perfectly orthodox in their acceptance of the doctrine of the Trinity, the Church and the Eucharist, and while they laid particular stress upon "conscious salvation" through an experience of "justification by faith," their "conversion" did not fundamentally change their theological outlook in other respects, as is revealed in their hymns, If the Church had given sympathetic guidance to their evangelical zeal and directed it, as in the thirteenth century the Papacy had the wisdom to use St. Francis and St. Dominic for its own purposes, the Methodist revival might have become a rallying point instead of a schism. But the bishops lacked the vision and understanding, and the parochial clergy and their congregations closed their churches to the preachers and evangelists, sometimes even forbidding their followers the use of the sacraments. It was this policy of repression and exclusion that drove the movement into Dissent as a counsel of despair.

Nevertheless, the fact remains that the revival had within it from the start the seeds of sectarianism absent in the Franciscan counterpart. Two strains met in the Wesleys, as we have seen, and from their Dissenting ancestry they inherited an individualism which found spiritual expression in their doctrine of rebirth interpreted in terms of justification and perfection, not easily reconcilable with the traditional conception of baptismal regeneration. If the two aspects of salvation are not actually contradictory, it required more subtlety of mind and theological knowledge than the founders possessed to bring them into juxtaposition. Sacramental sanctification was not denied but it was made subsidiary to individual personal conversion. Moreover, they had no appreciation of constitutional ecclesiastical order to which in theory they were committed by virtue of their position as duly commissioned ministers of the Word and sacraments in the Anglican Communion. Thus, as early as 1740 Charles Wesley set up a rival altar in a school at Kingswood where he gave Communion to his followers, and the same year an order of lay preachers was instituted to serve as permanent officers in the chapels established by the society as an independent community. It was only a matter of time before the sacraments were administered in them by ministers appointed by John Wesley, who as a duly ordained priest claimed for himself the right to delegate his office to others, and eventually, in 1784, to appoint Dr. Thomas Coke as "superintendent" in North America with episcopal status. Thus a schismatic denomination was created, officially described as "The People called Methodists," fully equipped with conventicles, a ministry and sacramental system of its own, a pastoral organization of societies, circuits, quarterly meetings, and an annual conference, which consolidated the connection as an integral entity.

The sectarian tendency did not even end here. As the movement grew and developed its membership was composed mainly of people who had never come under Anglican influences, or, as in the case of George Whitfield, who were more at home among Calvinists than Arminian Wesleyans. Therefore, the forces were soon divided on the question of predestination, just as John Wesley broke with the Moravians over the matter of mystical pietism. This caused the secession of the followers of Whitfield and the Countess of Huntingdon, who formed themselves into the Methodist New Connection in 1797, later merged in the United Methodist Church as a result of further schisms from the parent body in 1827, 1835 and 1849.[1] A bid for greater freedom in evangelistic work produced the Primitive Methodists in 1810 as a separate organization with its own conference, and out of it emerged in the 'sixties (1865) of the last century *The Salvation Army* under the leadership of one of its ministers, William Booth.

This remarkable movement, organized on a military basis as the name suggests, acquired an international scope directed chiefly to the evangelization of the poorest and most neglected section of society. Committed to combat vice, poverty and social and moral degradation in all its forms, it adopted a quasi-military discipline and engaged in an aggressive philanthropic and reforming campaign which has carried its devoted army of evangelists to all parts of the world. More definitely orthodox than the Society of Friends or the Unitarians, the Salvation Army vested its teaching on the divine inspiration of the Bible and proclaimed a theology of salvation based on the doctrine of the Fall and the universal call to repentance and justification by faith. It abandoned, however, the Methodist conception of institutional religion and in 1882 ceased to administer any sacraments. Although their efficacy in the scheme of salvation is questioned it is not denied that in particular cases the Sacrament may have

[1]The Welsh Calvinistic Methodists are a survival of this schism, the counterpart of the Countess of Huntingdon's Connection in England.

their uses, and permission is granted on occasions to resort to the sacramental ordinances of one or other of the Nonconformist bodies. The natural channel of grace, however, is through conversion issuing in a regenerated life.

The disunion which characterized Methodism in the heyday of its enthusiasm has now been stayed and the principal divisions and subdivisions of the communion have been consolidated in a single denomination under the comprehensive title of Methodism. This has been made possible because the schisms for the most part were administrative and governmental rather than doctrinal. Where there was a deeper breach in faith and practice, as for example, in the case of the Salvation Army, absorption in the parent body has not been effected. But progress has been made towards a wider amalgamation with Presbyterians and Congregationalists, while the historic affinities with Anglicanism make for a more sympathetic understanding between the two communions in their respective efforts towards reunion. The widespread use of the Book of Common Prayer, the acceptance of the creeds as the doctrinal basis of the faith, its conception of a visible Church and sacramental system, despite important divergences in order and discipline, place Methodism in much the same position as the connecting link between the Church of England and the Nonconformist Free Churches as that occupied by the Anglican Communion and the rest of Christendom, Catholic and Protestant.

THE CHURCH AND THE CHURCHES

In the sixteenth and seventeenth centuries Nonconformity was compelled to become sectarian willynilly, and long after the principle of religious toleration was recognized in this country the tendency persisted. This phase of the Reformation, however, now seems to have spent its force and is in process of returning to a wider conception of unification, isolation giving place to co-operation. As Christianity began as a sect of Nazarenes within Judaism and gradually assumed the proportions of a church, or *ecclesia*, with the Twelve Apostles as the original nucleus of the larger whole, so the separated congregations segregated from the rest of Christendom for the maintenance of particular doctrines and forms of government, are now less content to remain in isolation. Instead of glorying in their own distinctive characteristics as "Dissenters" or "Nonconformists," each distinguished from the other by clearly defined differentiations, to-day the principal reformed denominations regard themselves as a composite whole under the designation of "free churches."

Regarded from the Catholic standpoint, the Church is fundamentally a unity, not a multiplicity of congregations or churches. As the Visible Society founded by Christ to be the completion of the Jewish worshipping community, it is essentially one, holy, catholic and apostolic, as proclaimed in the Nicene Creed, called into being for the worship of the one God and pledged to teach and guard the one faith and extend throughout the world its one sacramental life through its apostolic ministry. To this organic unity it is irrevocably committed because upon it its union with Christ as its divine Head depends. But whether or not this essential unity is concentrated in a single supreme Pontiff as the sole Vicar of Christ on earth, is a matter of dispute between Roman Catholics on the affirmative side, and, on the other side, the Eastern Orthodox Church, the Old Catholics and the Anglicans, all of whom deny the claim. But apart from this very important differentiation, this Catholic conception of the Church was the doctrine, stated in general terms, to which the non-Anglican Protestant Reformers refused to conform because for them "the Church" had an entirely different significance, being composed primarily of fellowships of believers invisibly, subjectively and mystically united with Christ as the one and only source and channel of divine grace.

Differ as each group of congregations, or churches, might in mode of organization and theological emphasis, they were for the most part agreed in their bid for freedom alike from State control, credal allegiance and prescribed forms of worship. The situation, however, does not really admit of any generalization since Presbyterianism became virtually the Establishment as the official religion in Scotland while the Wesleyans repudiated neither the creeds nor the Prayer Book. Or, again, as the Church of England developed into the

I

Anglican Communion it was only in England that the State connection was maintained. Therefore, with the growth of toleration and a widened "œcumenical" outlook, a new spirit has arisen, and at long last, after centuries of divergence, a fresh effort is being made to mend the rents in the seamless robe of Christ. The conception of a "Universal Church" with ministries and organizations operating "within their several spheres" is replacing that of the segregation of separated, self-contained and mutually exclusive congregations of believers. This is brought out clearly by Dr. Newton Flew, the President of the Methodist Conference, in his book, *Jesus and the Church*, where the Church is represented as the earthly body of the risen Lord through whose members He carries on His work in the world. "In the first place it is the object of the divine activity, and then the organ or instrument of God's saving purpose for mankind." What precisely is the relation of the somewhat nebulous "Universal Church" to the historic Catholic Church has yet to be determined, but that thought is moving along these lines towards the reunion of Christendom under its one divine Head is a cause for profound thankfulness and hope. The vision is for many days and its realization will only be accomplished by successive stages after a thorough, fearless and protracted consideration of the fundamental causes and occasions of the divisions that have transformed Christianity into a city of confusion for the last four hundred years.

While the so-called "œcumenical outlook"[1] is to be welcomed, the history of the Church in England should be a warning against any attempt to repeat the policy of the Elizabethan Settlement. Genuine and permanent union will never be secured by ambiguously phrased statements of belief and practice which gloss over fundamental differences in the cardinal doctrines of the Faith. While in the light of present-day theological and historical knowledge many of the most controversial issues in the sixteenth century are now capable of a very different interpretation, enough has been recorded in the foregoing pages to show that the divergencies in faith

[1] The term "œcumenical" is now applied to a movement working for the reunion of separated Christians in full loyalty to their own traditions.

and order are very deeply laid, extending in some cases to the Person and Work of Christ and the Being of God. It is unrealistic to suppose that such a cleavage, deepened and widened by centuries of controversy, can be restored by filling the dividing gap with very loosely cemented rubble. Language can be as deceptive to-day as it was in the more literary sixteenth century. For example, the "historic episcopate" at the time of the Reformation, when it was a primary cause of Nonconformity, may require a very different interpretation to restore it to its original functions and meaning, as is suggested in a recent illuminating study of the problem by a group of Anglo-Catholic scholars under the leadership of Dr. K. E. Kirk, Bishop of Oxford (cf. *The Apostolic Ministry*, 1946), and when this is accomplished it may again become a unifying force in Christendom. But until the institution is admitted, and its precise significance determined and accepted by all the parties concerned, it is building upon sand to try to erect upon this foundation an enduring edifice. It is not the historic episcopate but what the office signifies that is the crucial issue. To call "moderators" "bishops" does not solve the problem, any more than to camouflage the doctrinal difference between a "priest" and "pastor" by the non-committal term "presbyter." The same applies to the conception of the Church, the sacraments and the creeds. When agreement upon these cardinal verities is reached questions of order, liturgy, discipline and organization can be adjusted as circumstances require, as has been accomplished in the recent Methodist amalgamations, or in the negotiations between the Anglican Communion and the Old Catholics. Failure to face these facts will only lead to new schisms and a deeper rift between Catholic and Protestant Christendom.

If the aim of the œcumenical movement is the reunion of Christendom as a whole—and nothing less can fulfil the Gospel precept of Christian unity—it must be all-embracing. To bring together the non-episcopal denominations in a closer fellowship and effect a union of them with the Anglican Church (and possibly some other non-papal communions) doubtless would be an important step towards the final goal, provided that it did not resolve Christendom into a sharply divided dualism comparable in the political sphere to an Anglo-Saxon Western *bloc* of nations opposed to a Slav *bloc* screened by an iron curtain. For good or ill the Papacy has been the most powerful unifying and disruptive force in Christendom, and it still maintains the allegiance of the major portion of those who profess and call themselves Christians. This vast jurisdiction and tremendous international force numbers some four hundred million adherents (many of whom are phenomenal for their zeal and devotion) and is distributed throughout the four quarters of the globe, of whom over twenty millions occur in the British Empire. To ignore its significance would be as ridiculous as eliminating the Prince of Denmark in the production of *Hamlet*. Therefore, it is to the place and function of Roman Catholicism in this complex situation that we must now turn our attention.

BIBLIOGRAPHY

PRESBYTERIANISM

Balfour of Burleigh, *The Rise and Development of Presbyterianism in Scotland*. Cambridge, 1911.

Cox, J. T., *Practice and Procedure of the Church of Scotland*. Edinburgh and London, 1945.

Drysdale, A. H., *History of Presbyterians in England*. London, 1889.

Gillett, E. H., *History of the Presbyterian Church in the United States*. Philadelphia, 1864.

Ogilvie, J. N., *The Presbyterian Churches*. London, 1925.

CONGREGATIONALISM

Burrage, C., *The Early History of English Dissenters in the Light of Recent Research*. Cambridge, 1912.

Dale, R. W., *History of English Congregationalism*. London, 1907 (with good bibliography).

Dexter, H. M., *Congregationalism of the Last Three Hundred Years as seen in its Literature*. New York, 1880.

Powicke, F. J., "The Congregational Churches" in *Evangelical Christianity*. Ed. W. B. Selbie. London, 1911.

Selbie, W. B., *Congregationalism*. Ed. L. P. Jacks. London, 1928.

Walker, Williston, *The Creeds and Platforms of Congregationalism*. London, 1895.

BAPTIST CHURCHES

Carlile, J. C., *The Story of the English Baptists*. Edinburgh, 1905.

Newman, A. H., *A History of the Baptist Churches in the United States*. Philadelphia, 1915.

Rushbrooke, J. H., *The Baptist Movement on the Continent of Europe*. London, 1923.

Vedder, H. C., *History of the Baptists*. London, 1892 (Philadelphia, 1907).

Whitley, W. T., *A History of British Baptists*. London, 1923.

SOCIETY OF FRIENDS

Barclay, R., *An Apology for the True Christian Divinity*. English Translation, 1678.

Braithwaite, W. C., *The Beginnings of Quakerism*. London, 1923. *The Second Period of Quakerism*. London, 1911.

Fox, G., *The Journal of George Fox*. Ed. N. Penney. 2 vols. Cambridge, 1911. (Reproduced in one volume in Everyman's Library.)

Graham, J. W., *The Faith of a Quaker*. Cambridge, 1920.

Grubb, E., *Quaker Thought and History*. Swarthmore Press, 1925.

Jones, R. M., *The Later Periods of Quakerism*. London, 1921.

Nuttall, G. F., *The Holy Spirit in Puritan Faith and Experience*. Oxford, Blackwell, 1947, for an account of the issue between the Puritans and the Quakers.

Swarthmore Lectures. A series of Quaker literature.

UNITARIANS

Carpenter, J. E., *Freedom and Truth: Modern Views of Unitarian Christianity*. London, 1925.

Gordon, A., *Heads of English Unitarian History*. London, 1895.

Lindsey, T., *Historical View of the State of the Unitarian Doctrine and Worship from the Reformation*. 1783.

Martineau, J., *A Seat of Authority in Religion*. London, 1890.

METHODISM

Abbey, C. J., and Overton, J. H., *The English Church in the Eighteenth Century*. 2 vols. London, 1896.

Dixon, J., *Methodism in America*. London, 1849.

Eayrs, G., *John Wesley, Christian, Philosopher and Church Founder*. London, 1926.

Flew, R. N., *Jesus and His Church*. London, 1938. (2nd Edition, 1943).

Gregory, J. R., *A History of Methodism*. 2 vols. London, 1911.

Kendall, H. B., *The Origin and History of the Primitive Methodist Church*. London, 1905.

Peake, A. S., "Methodism" in *Evangelical Christianity*. London, 1911.

Piette, M., *John Wesley in the Evolution of Protestantism*. London, 1937. (A sympathetic study by a Roman Catholic writer, with a foreword by H. B. Workman and Bishop F. C. Kelley.)

Rigg, J. H., *The Living Wesley*. London, 1868.

Simon, J., *The Revival of Religion in England in the Eighteenth Century*. London, 1907.

Townsend, W. J., Workman, J., and Eayrs, G., *A New History of Methodism*. London, 1909.

Tyerman, L., *Life and Times of Wesley*. London, 1870–1.

SALVATION ARMY

Beglie, H., *Life of William Booth*. London, 1919.

Booth, W., *In Darkest England and the Way Out*. London, 1890.

Nicol, A. M., *General Booth and the Salvation Army*. London, 1911.

The literature of Nonconformity is so enormous that only a typical selection can be given under each of the above headings. Full bibliographies will be found appended to the appropriate articles in Hastings's *Encyclopædia of Religion and Ethics* and *The Encyclopædia Britannica*. The most comprehensive survey of the period and the history of Nonconformity will be found in J. Stoughton's *History of Religion in England* (8 vols. London, 1901). *English Dissent under the Hanoverians*, by D. Coomer (London, 1947) is a very much slighter popular study of English Dissent under George I and George II containing an excellent bibliography. For an annotated and classified bibliography of the literature on reunion *see* H. R. T. Brandreth, *Unity and Reunion* (London, 1946).

CHAPTER VII

ROMAN CATHOLICISM SINCE THE REFORMATION

THE movement known as the Reformation usually is regarded as a Protestant reaction against the Medieval Church and the Renaissance Papacy. This, of course, is true but it is often forgotten that there was also a Counter-Reformation, or Catholic revival, which coincided with and arose out of the same set of circumstances that produced the more radical revolt against the papal jurisdiction. It was, in fact, only Eastern Christendom that escaped the ecclesiastical upheaval in the sixteenth century and pursued its course in complete isolation from the turmoil of events in the West, with all the subsequent currents and cross-currents of modern thought, new learning and cultural development. Western Europe was too deeply involved in a complex situation, partly social and partly religious, for any institution to remain unaffected by the revolutionary movements that were shattering the whole structure of society, and changing fundamentally the outlook of all sections and classes in the community.

As early as the time of the Crusades and the Moorish invasion of Spain and France, new influences were gradually undermining the old static and complacent solidarity through culture contact and new experiences. A new sense of national spirit was arising coupled with a greater consciousness of social injustices, finding expression eventually in the Peasants' Revolt of 1524, while in the intellectual sphere the scientific method was struggling to come to birth in such pioneers as Nicholas of Cusa (1401–54), Copernicus (1473–1543), Giordano Bruno (1518–1600) and Francis Bacon (1561–1639), culminating in René Descartes (1595–1650). And it was in Italy, and not least in the city of Rome itself, that Renaissance Humanism was entrenched. Even the Vatican, rebuilt by Nicholas V between 1447 and 1455 to be the greatest palace

135

in the world and the finest cultural centre, was steeped in the new civilization with its pagan antecedents. And as patrons of the arts the popes of the period were unsurpassed. The papal court had become the most luxurious and gorgeous establishment in Europe, and desire for beautiful buildings, magnificent gardens and cultivated conversation completely eclipsed the earlier medieval ideals of asceticism and the evangelical counsels of perfection as the highest good. To make Rome and Florence the finest cities on earth surpassed all the wishful dreams of a New Jerusalem in planes of being other than physical. The arts should be lavishly employed to adorn churches and cathedrals, as well as other public buildings, not primarily for the greater glory of God, as in the Middle Ages, but because so adorned they were a fitting environment for cultivated minds.

THE COUNTER-REFORMATION

Since it was at the heart and centre of the Western Church that these ideals and aspirations prevailed, the time was ripe for far-reaching reforms in the Holy See itself as well as in the body politic. But serious and deeply laid as were the religious and ecclesiastical evils of the times, they were by no means irremedial within the existing framework of the Papacy, and it is to the credit and wisdom of the Church that it made a strenuous effort to set its house in order. After the Treaty of Noyon in 1510 the Papal States were consolidated and steps soon were taken to deal with open scandals. In his opening sermon at the fifth Lateran Council two years later, Egidius of Viterbo urged the need of reform and the recovery of the lost ideals of sanctity. The plea, however, fell on deaf ears, and the failure of the Council to deal effectively with the prevailing moral and spiritual bankruptcy of the Papacy was a contributory cause of Luther's revolt against ecclesiastical authority as a whole. But before he raised his standard there was a growing urge in Italy for effective action against the inveterate abuses which the challenge in Germany made irresistible.

It now became apparent that if Catholic orthodoxy was to be maintained the Faith must be vindicated, and at least some of the blatant evils, such as pluralism and non-residence, removed. Greater care must be taken in the selection and training of candidates for the priesthood, and the authority of the Church strengthened. To these ends a Council was assembled at Trent on 15th March, 1545, and remained in session for more than eighteen years. If no attempt was made to effect a reconciliation between the Church and its Protestant opponents, or to determine precisely the relation of the episcopate to the Papacy, indulgence preachers (*quæstors*) were abolished, the standard of clerical education was raised, and the cardinal doctrines of the Faith were defined in terms which have remained the official dogmatic basis of Roman Catholicism to the present day. As the German scholar Harnack has said, "the Medieval Church went forth from the Council of Trent still substantially the ancient Church," but it went forth strengthened by a reaffirmation of its faith, unity and totality, purified of some of its abuses, and with a determination to carry out its mission in and to the world with a renewed zeal and efficiency. It is not surprising, therefore, that the Counter-Reformation gave rise to the foundation of new Religious Orders (e.g., Jesuits, Capuchins, Oratorians, Ursulines, etc.) to engage in this task.

The Jesuits

The hour produced the man in the person of Ignatius Loyola (*c.* 1491–1556), who realized the need of a higher standard of devotional life among the clergy and a new conception of the monastic vocation. His *Spiritual Exercises*, which took shape during his sojourn in a cave near Manresa, in Spain, were intended in the first instance as a manual of spiritual training to be put into practice during retreat with a view to the conquest of self and the ordering of the life of the retreatant according to the will of God "without being influenced in one's decision by any inordinate affection." The retreat, it was assumed, would be made either to consider the question of vocation and to choose whether it be in the priesthood, the religious state, or in the ordinary life in the world; or to reform, if need be, and to order his life in the state already chosen and fixed; or simply to renew and deepen the devout life of grace. The influence of the "Exercises" on

Catholic piety has been immense, and the Ignatian method has been widely adopted by the conductors of retreats ever since it was first devised. But it was the new Jesuit order which Ignatius created in 1534 that was destined to have the most profound effect on the subsequent history of the Roman Communion.

The Society of Jesus began as an Order of very highly trained and wholly devoted men living under the threefold vow of poverty, chastity and obedience and pledged to a rigid military discipline based on the *Spiritual Exercises* (i.e., a literal following of Christ in a life of renunciation and devotion as set forth particularly in the two great meditations on "The Kingdom of Christ" and "The Two Standards"). When the conversion of the heathen proved to be impracticable, the society was placed unreservedly at the service of the Holy See, thereby avoiding any possible developments in a sectarian direction. After its constitution had been officially accepted and approved by Paul III in 1540 it concentrated upon preaching, pastoral visitation, and the teaching of youth. Fortitude, loyalty and absolute obedience have been its characteristic features from the beginning, inculcated in the rigorous training of novices prolonged over a period perhaps of twelve years and renewed year by year after full profession when "the Exercises" are "made" in the annual retreat.

The success of the venture has been only equalled by the opposition it has encountered, and this by no means entirely from its opponents outside the Church. Before the death of the founder in 1556 a thousand Jesuits were distributed over twelve different provinces in Europe, and the society was well on its way towards becoming one of the most powerful influences in the Counter-Reformation, both in the struggle against protestantism and in the propagation of the Faith throughout the world by missionaries of the calibre of Francis Xavier in India and Japan. Organized under the supreme control of a Superior General, its government was and always has been essentially monarchical, based on a military type of discipline. An iron rule of this nature readily becomes a tyranny, just as whole-hearted loyalty to a cause is liable to have recourse to questionable methods in the attainment of worthy ends, especially when a subtle casuistry is adopted. And the Jesuits fell victims to both these snares. By their constitution they were Ultramontanes[1]—a term applied to those who support the absolute supremacy of the Papacy and the centralization of all ecclesiastical government and dogmatic teaching in the occupant of the Holy See. They also upheld the principle known as probabilism, according to which when it is only probable and not certain that a particular ecclesiastical precept or law applies to a particular case, in hearing confessions it is lawful and right to give the penitent the benefit of the doubt if the reasons are serious, even though they be less serious than the reasons for a stricter course. This not unreasonable principle was extended by the so-called "laxists" to cover cases where an element of doubt could be introduced by almost any method, and, therefore, became liable to grave abuse on the part of highly-trained confessors like the Jesuits, skilled in the art of subtle reasoning.

It was in these two ways, through its ultramontanism and its casuistry, that the society came into conflict with the Nationalist, or Gallican, movement in France associated with the names of Jansen, Blaise Pascal, and the Cistercian convent of Port Royal. The complicated controversy that ensued, turning as it did upon papal jurisdiction and prerogatives, and the absolute claims of a strict moral integrity (connected by the Gallicans with St. Augustine's doctrine of divine grace) lies outside our present inquiry. But the cleavage between the Ultramontanes and the Gallicans had repercussions which were felt in England, where a liaison was attempted between the Anglican Church and the followers of Jansen in France through the intervention of William Wake, chaplain to the English envoy in Paris, and afterwards Archbishop of Canterbury (1716), and a French theologian, Dupin, whose overtures were supported by the Cardinal Archbishop of Paris, de Noailles. The Jesuits, however, frustrated the venture, and after the death of Dupin in 1719 the negotiations ceased; Gallicanism in the meantime having

[1]Literally the word means "beyond the mountains," and therefore was used by Catholics north of the Alps, especially in France in the seventeenth century, to describe the policy of the centralization of administration in Rome, and the doctrinal implications of this constitution.

become eclipsed as a result of the combined efforts of the King, Louis XV, and his confessor Le Tellier, a Jesuit, who in all probability was responsible for the final condemnation of Jansenism by the bull *Unigenitus*, published by Clement XI on 8th September, 1713. It was only in Holland that the movement survived in a small and struggling community at Utrecht, which was subsequently constituted as a separate church, called Old Catholics, after the excommunication of Döllinger and his followers for rejecting the doctrine of papal infallibility promulgated in 1870.[1]

ROMAN CATHOLICISM IN ENGLAND

By the beginning of the eighteenth century the remarkable revival of post-Tridentine Catholicism had reached its peak and a rapid decline set in with the triumph of rationalism and the "Enlightenment" in the world of thought, and the growth of absolutism on the part of secular rulers. In England the reaction against the Papacy hardened after the ignominious flight and exile of James II, and even the Non-jurors looked away from Rome towards the Eastern Orthodox Church for a possible liaison. Except in Lancashire, Yorkshire and the western highlands of Scotland, where Roman Catholicism was deeply rooted despite the penal laws, it was only in a few isolated places that the seed sown by Edmund Campion and the Jesuit missionaries from Douai and Rheims in the reign of Elizabeth survived. In London it was kept alive in the eighteenth century mainly by six chapels attached to foreign embassies, but in Ireland more rapid progress was made so that by the middle of the century it was firmly established notwithstanding restrictive and oppressive legislation.

In the reign of James II England had been divided into four districts under a Vicar Apostolic appointed by the Holy See, and this organization persisted during the reaction after the revolution of 1689. The community, however, was very small and it was not until the second half of the century that the growing tolerance of the age ameliorated the lot of what was unquestionably an unpopular minority, regarded as

[1]A measure of intercommunion has now been established between the Old Catholics and the Church of England.

politically dangerous on account of its foreign allegiances and contacts. To allay these fears the Duke of Norfolk and nine other Roman Catholic peers, together with 163 commoners, presented a loyal address to George III in 1778 affirming the attachment of the community to the civil constitution of the realm and the Crown in the person of the reigning monarch. This brought the first Relief Act repealing some of the restrictive measures of the Statute of 1699, and permitting an oath of allegiance which did not conflict with the Faith. The George Gordon Riot, however, which occurred in 1780, fostered by the Protestant Association, showed the antipapal feeling that was still predominant in the country. Roman Catholic chapels and residences of the clergy and laity were wrecked by a fanatical mob, and the saintly Vicar Apostolic, Richard Challoner, who was nearly ninety years of age, had to flee from his rooms in London. But it was men like Challoner who kept the flag flying and by their steadfastness, devotion, piety and zeal commended "the old religion" by example as well as by precept.

The Counter-Reformation does not appear to have had very much influence on English Roman Catholicism at this period. Thus, Challoner's *Meditations for Every Day in the Year* and his *Garden of the Soul*, in its original form, were singularly free from post-Tridentine Ultramontane doctrines and devotions, and it is significant that in their "protestation" to the government in 1789, the Roman Catholic bishops, after denying that they and their flock owed obedience to the Papacy or to General Councils which obliged them to take up arms against the realm or subvert its laws, went on to declare that they acknowledged "no infallibility in the Pope," and neither apprehended nor believed that their "disobedience to any such orders or decrees (should any such be given or made) could subject them to any punishment whatever." Dr. Matthew Gibson subsequently withdrew his signature from the document, but England at this period was too isolated from the Continent for Ultramontanism to have become a live issue. Events, however, on the other side of the Channel were reaching a climax in the French Revolution which required an all-powerful infallible Papacy to meet the forces opposed to the Church and restore the Faith after the reign of terror. This, men like Joseph de Maistre, the Vicomte de Bonald, Lacordaire and Lamennais, were not slow to recognize. Gallican nationalistic Erastianism had suffered a mortal blow and Ultramontanism was in the ascendant, notwithstanding cleavages among its supporters.

THE GROWTH OF ULTRAMONTANISM

The repercussions of these reactions were felt in England. In 1793 Douai had been seized by the revolutionary government and with the closing of the English seminaries in France some eight thousand refugees found their way into Britain. Funds were raised for their support by parliamentary grants and private subscription, and if many returned after the Concordat with the Vatican concluded by Napoleon in 1802, some remained. Moreover, a new link with the Continent had been forged, and it was only a question of time before Ultramontanism, carried along by the force of nineteenth-century Romanticism, reached Britain. If the Church was to regain her predominance in the temporal sphere and provide the spiritual dynamic of the new civilization that was emerging in Western Europe, the ideal of medieval Christendom must be recovered. This seemed to suggest the re-establishment of Rome as the consolidating and unifying centre with the Pope as the sovereign ruler and guardian of the liberties of the subject against the tyranny of an omnipotent secular authority as exemplified by revolutionary France and the secularized German and Austrian States, where the policy of Joseph II between 1765–90 had brought the Church under civic control, especially in the operation of papal bulls and the institution of national seminaries under State supervision.

The suppression of the Jesuits by Clement XIV in 1773 coincided with the growth of German nationalism and the Erastian movement that came to be called Josephism. This was reinforced by the current German political philosophy, but the unpopularity of the régime gave the Ultramontanes their opportunity to promote a Catholic revival in the cause of liberty, which found support first in Protestant Prussia and later spread to the Catholic States. A schism, however, occurred in the middle of the century in Bavaria when Ignatius von Döllinger (1799–1890), who during his tenure of the Chair of Canon Law and Church History at Munich, opposed the revival of scholasticism by the Jesuits in the German college in Rome, and their Romanizing influence in the seminaries in Germany. Taking his stand against the temporal power and the autocracy of the Papacy, he became the leader of a group of scholars and bishops who shared his alarm at the growing papal prerogatives and the reactionary attitude of Ultramontanism towards the scientific and philosophic thought of the age.

Among those who came under his stimulating influence was John Lord Acton (1834–1902), a distinguished member of an old English Roman Catholic family who had taken up their residence in Naples and become naturalized Italian subjects. As a boy he had been educated at Oscott College, Birmingham, where Monseignor Wiseman, afterwards Cardinal Archbishop of Westminster, was then the president, and who had been for many years on intimate terms with Döllinger. In 1850 Acton went to Munich as a student and stayed with the professor. This was the beginning of a life-long friendship and an introduction to the continental Ultramontane controversy. After visiting France with Döllinger and meeting the most eminent historical scholars there and in Germany, he returned to England nine years later and entered Parliament as a Liberal. Through the medium of a Roman Catholic journal, *The Rambler* (later transformed into a quarterly periodical under the title of *Home and Foreign Review*) he introduced the theological position of the Munich school to English readers, while William George Ward represented the Ultramontane standpoint in *The Dublin Review*.

By this time the English Roman Catholic community had ceased to be a small ostracized and persecuted minority. Its political emancipation in 1829 gave it a legitimate place in the religious structure of the nation, and under the leadership of Nicholas Wiseman the country was organized as a "missionary" province with its own hierarchy of twelve suffragan sees under himself as metropolitan Archbishop of Westminster.

Opposition of course had had to be encountered and overcome both from Protestant agitation from without and suspicions from within, mainly on the part of the clergy and laity who feared that his desire for "an influx of fresh blood" meant the introduction of continental Ultramontane innovations. Wiseman himself was a man of balanced judgment but the Oxford Movement in the Church of England produced converts who brought with them all the zeal of a newly-found faith. Having forsaken what seemed to them to be a city of confusion and made their submission to the Holy See, in some instances at a very considerable personal sacrifice, they were hardly likely to be lukewarm in their attitude to the burning question of papal infallibility and all that this doctrine involved in the middle of the nineteenth century.

Thus, W. G. Ward, Fellow and Tutor of Balliol College, Oxford, was the leader of the Roman Party in the Anglican Catholic Revival initiated by Keble in 1833 (cf. pp. 161), and in his provocative book *The Ideal of a Christian Church*, in 1844 before his secession he had declared that "the Roman Church, and only the Roman Church, satisfies the condition of what a Church ought to be." For a while it is true he maintained the anomalous position of holding "all Roman doctrine" and at the same time retaining his membership of the Anglican Communion. But this not surprisingly proved to be only a temporary expedient. Within a year he was received into the papal jurisdiction, and, as was to be expected, he became a protagonist of the Ultramontane tradition against the Munich school.

The case of John Henry Newman (1801–90), whose secession followed immediately that of Ward, was rather different in its background and sequel. Newman had been brought up under Calvinistic influences and himself passed through an experience of conversion at the age of fifteen. As an undergraduate at Trinity College, Oxford, he retained his evangelical allegiances until, after election to a Fellowship at Oriel in 1822, he joined a group of liberal-minded scholars (known as Noetics). This broadened his outlook, while his subsequent association with the brilliant coterie of Fellows, who, in reaction against Noetic liberalism and Anglican Erastianism, were seeking a confirmation of the Laudian tradition in the Early Christian Fathers, led him to an appreciation of the value of Catholic continuity in Christianity.

It was not long, however, before doubts began to arise in his mind. Not being rooted and grounded in Anglicanism like Keble and Pusey and most of the Oriel Tractarian group, as opposition increased it seemed to Newman that a disconcerting parallel existed between the position of Eutyches, a heretic of the fifth century, and that of the contemporary Church of England. This was confirmed by a similar analogy between Anglicanism and the Donatist schism in the Early Church, suggested by Wiseman in *The Dublin Review*, in which St. Augustine's judgment against the schismatics was quoted with deadly effect—"the whole world judges right." Thus, he began to wonder whether a National Church like the Communion he had extolled as the *via media*, could be trusted to maintain the true faith, cut off as it was from the main stream of Western Catholic Christendom. As he remarked, "he had seen a ghost," and henceforth he could never be as though he had not seen it. Two years later the spectre reappeared and completed its work. In 1841 he published the ninetieth of the famous "Tracts for the Times" issued by the Oriel group, in which he argued that the Thirty-nine Articles strictly interpreted did not contradict the official teaching of the Roman Church as set forth at the Council of Trent. It was only the pre-Tridentine superstitions in the *doctrina Romanensium* that were condemned.

As a matter of historical fact the argument was valid within certain limits, but the storm of protest it produced carried Newman into the papal jurisdiction and divided the Tractarians into two camps—the one maintaining the High Church Anglican tradition of Hooker, Laud and the Caroline divines, the other looking more and more towards continental Ultramontanism. Newman retired to his quasi-monastic retreat at Littlemore until on a blustering day (9th October) in the autumn of 1845 he was received into "the One Fold of Christ," as it seemed to him, by an Italian Passionist, Father Dominic. After a stay at Oscott under Wiseman, he went to Rome the following year to be ordained to the priesthood and

K

then joined the Congregation of the Oratory, founded by St. Philip Neri in the sixteenth century. In 1847 he established an Oratorian house at Edgbaston, Birmingham, where except for a brief period in Ireland, he spent the rest of his life.

From this obscure refuge Newman's influence was felt throughout the Catholic world, though he had to encounter considerable opposition, ranging from a slanderous and ill-founded attack by Charles Kingsley to the perpetual mis-representations of Manning (who succeeded Wiseman as Archbishop of Westminster) and the irresponsible Ward. Both went much farther than Newman was prepared to follow in the direction of extreme Ultramontanism, though he was never in doubt about the doctrine of papal infallibility. In his Anglican days the idea of an infallible living Church had captured his imagination and led him to see in the development of Christian doctrine an organic evolutionary process that reached its goal and climax in the Papacy. Indeed, in his own field of theology he had the distinction of anticipating by nearly twenty years the enunciation of the principle which Darwin applied to the origin of species. But, nevertheless, at the end of his life, as the Vatican Council of 1870 approached, he was alive to the dangers of "a tendency towards excessive centralization," and brought all the weight of his influence to bear on the framing of a definition of the doctrine of infallibility in terms which might not appear to the world to sanction the extravagances of the extreme Ultramontane position, which he believed to be at variance with traditional Catholic theology. It is probable, in fact, that the decree in its final form owed something to his counsels. At any rate, when he saw it as it was passed he expressed his satisfaction at the results of the council, and defended the definition against the onslaughts of Gladstone.

THE IMMACULATE CONCEPTION

That an *ex cathedra* statement on the part of the Church concerning the precise nature, significance and jurisdiction of the Pope was essential had become clear by the middle of the nineteenth century, and careful preparations were made in Rome for the consideration of the issue and the declaration of an official pronouncement. Moreover, the political situation demanded drastic action on the part of the Holy See. The temporal rule of the Papacy was menaced by the rising tide of nationalism in Italy, and the establishment of a kingdom under Victor Emmanuel through the intervention of Garibaldi in 1861 had its inevitable sequel in the loss of the papal States, reducing Pius to the spectacular but ignominious position of a "prisoner of the Vatican." Thus ended the dream of Hildebrand with a sad awakening for the occupant of the chair of St. Peter. In this desperate plight his thoughts turned to the Blessed Mother of God, very much as in ancient Rome, just before the decisive battle that ended the Punic Wars, recourse was made to the sibylline oracle which recommended that the holy stone, the symbol of the Great Mother of Phrygia, should be brought to the city, where her cultus was established on the Palatine in 191 B.C.

The doctrine of the Immaculate Conception of the Virgin Mary was first proclaimed by some English monks between 1121 and 1130 to reconcile her generation with the Augustinian theory of original sin, and to legitimatize the observance of the Feast of her Conception held on 8th December, which had been introduced into England and Ireland, probably from the East, before the Norman Conquest. The dogma, however, was refuted by the leading scholars of the thirteenth century, including Peter Lombard, Albertus Magnus, Bonaventura and St. Thomas Aquinas; and it was not until the next century, when the Augustinian position in the matter of unregenerated human depravity and the inheritance of concupiscence through sexual generation had been modified, that Duns Scotus and the Franciscans defended it against their Thomist rivals, the Dominicans. From then onwards the doctrine steadily gained ground in the universities as well as in popular devotion. In 1476 Sixtus IV adopted the Feast without officially endorsing the theological interpretations that had been placed upon it. The Council of Trent affirmed that its decree on original sin did not include "the Blessed and Immaculate Virgin Mary," and from the sixteenth century legends and spurious papal decrees were employed by the Jesuits and the other Ultramontanes to bolster up the dogma.

Therefore, the ground was well prepared for a formal promulgation at the psychological moment when supernatural aid was desperately needed to save the threatened Papal States and the temporal sovereignty of the Vatican. The absence of any reasonable Scriptural evidence in support of the contention was easily overcome in the uncritical circles in which the discussions were held by the analogical interpretation of passages of Holy Writ, many of which, as some of those present recognized, were wholly irrelevant. Consequently, after taking consultation with the bishops, on 8th December (the controversial Feast) 1854, Pius, in the presence of an august assembly of cardinals and other ecclesiastics, issued the bull *Ineffabilis*, in which he declared, pronounced and defined that "the doctrine which holds that the Most Blessed Virgin Mary, from the first instant of her conception was, by a most singular grace and privilege of Almighty God, in view of the merits of Jesus Christ, the Redeemer of the human race, preserved from all stain of original sin, is a doctrine revealed by God and therefore to be firmly and steadfastly believed by all the faithful."

THE SYLLABUS AND THE VATICAN COUNCIL

The promulgation of this decree carried with it as a corollary the dogma of papal infallibility, of which, in fact, it was an anticipation. As a means of staving off the political crisis the expedient was less successful than its prototype in 201 B.C., and the exigencies of the times required a further assertion of papal prerogatives to balance the vacillating policy of Pius IX. Therefore, in 1864 a *Syllabus of Errors* was published denouncing the separation of Church and State, secular education, and, except where Roman Catholicism was a minority as in Eastern Europe and England, the tolerance of freedom of conscience and religious teaching inconsistent with Roman orthodoxy, which, of course, now included the doctrine of the Immaculate Conception and other post-Tridentine Ultramontane innovations. Thus, in principle, and where possible in practice, the Catholic religion as interpreted and received by the Holy Roman and Apostolic Church, should be regarded as the only religion of the State to the exclusion of all other sects, schisms and jurisdictions. This declaration of policy was based on the assumption that Christendom is virtually co-terminous with the sovereign rule of the Supreme Pontiff, who could not be expected to make terms with, or even recognize, the liberalism that was challenging his absolutism.

To consolidate and define this Ultramontane position it was decided to convoke an Œcumenical Council at Rome, though the precise purpose of the assembly was not revealed until the policy had been carefully established and safeguarded. Nevertheless, notwithstanding the strength of the infallibilist majority, of which Manning, the English Archbishop of Westminster, was one of the most ardent and extreme members, a small but formidable minority existed, determined to fight a losing battle if not to the death at least until it reached the last ditch. This included such prominent prelates as Dupanloup, Bishop of Orleans, Ketteler, the *doyen* of the German episcopate, Haynald, Archbishop of Kalocsa in Hungary, Scherr of Munich, the Archbishops of Paris, Lyons and Milan; some of whom opposed the project on grounds of expediency, others on those of theological principle. That they were able to obtain considerable modification of the original proposal put forth and maintained throughout the negotiations by the Manning group of extreme Ultramontanes with the support of the Pope, is a testimony to their persistence. The final declaration, however, was clearly the triumph of papal absolutism set forth in terms which admit of no possible misunderstanding of their meaning and significance.

Thus, on 18th July, 1870, amid heavy rolling of thunder and vivid flashing of lightning, in the presence of a vast concourse of cardinals and patriarchs, primates and archbishops, bishops and abbots, assembled in the great basilica under the patronage of St. Peter the Prince of the Apostles, the Supreme Pontiff as his successor and Vicar of Christ on earth, gained assent, with only two abstentions, to a constitution which gave him and his successors complete and absolute jurisdictionary authority over the whole Church, not simply in matters of faith and morality, but also in questions touching discipline and government. "When the Roman bishop speaks *ex cathedra*, that is to say, when in performing his office as pastor and teacher of all Christians in virtue of his supreme apostolic authority, he defines a doctrine regarding faith or morals to be held by the whole Church, by the divine assistance promised to him in blessed Peter, is possessed of that infallibility with which the divine Redeemer willed that His Church should be endowed; and that for this reason, definitions of the Roman Pontiff of that kind are irreformable of themselves and not as a consequence of the consent of the Church."

By the adoption of this decree, called *Pastor Aeternus*, Roman Catholics everywhere, and apparently for all time, have been committed to these far-reaching and all-embracing claims. In a sense they were inherent in the institution from the time when it first adopted and developed the prerogatives and privileges of the *Pontifex Maximus* of the old imperial capital, and eventually endeavoured to establish a Holy Roman Empire in which the Church was deemed to have supreme authority not only in the spiritual but also in the secular sphere. But the opposition of the anti-infallibilist minority and their sympathizers outside the Council shows that the Ultramontane position was by no means universally accepted. Döllinger and his followers deliberately went into schism as "Old Catholics" and continued an episcopal succession through the Jansenist line of bishops of Utrecht to which reference has been made. The rest acquiesced in what seemed to them to be the prevailing voice of the Church regarded as the Mystical Body of Christ, "mother and mistress of all churches."

That "it is the Papacy that makes the papist," as C. K. Chesterton has aptly remarked, has been true ever since the Petrine claims were promulgated, but after 1870 the authoritarianism of Rome and the personal infallibility of its bishop as shepherd and teacher of all Christians, became a theological dogma with much wider and deeper implications than heretofore; dominating every aspect of human thought and activity that can in any sense be brought within the sphere of faith, morals and jurisdiction. As there is "one Lord, one faith, one baptism," so there is one Church under one Supreme Head and Pontiff who is invested with the absolute supernatural powers and authority which, it is alleged, were conferred on the Prince of the Apostles. To exercise private judgment against the will and decree of this infallible source of all wisdom is anathematized in the decree, but the attempt of the Manning party to make the Holy See a divine oracle to give a final answer to every relevant question that might arise failed. Indeed, it is by no means clear whether in fact an *ex cathedra* utterance fulfilling all the conditions of an infallible declaration, has ever been made since the Vatican Council claimed and defined the power, notwithstanding the urgent need for spiritual and ethical authoritative guidance the world has desperately needed in the intervening period with its two cosmic upheavals.

If the dogma is somewhat nebulous in its practical significance and application, unquestionably it provides a firm basis which all other interpretations of Christianity lack. As Dr. A. E. J. Rawlinson has pointed out, "there is a recurrent type of mind which is fundamentally sceptical and distrustful of reason, and yet craving religious certitude and peace, which will gravitate always towards Rome; and for minds of this type it is probable that only the Roman Communion is in the long run in a position to cater. The demand for such souls is not for any form of strictly rational or verifiable authority. It is for authority in the form of a purely external and oracular guarantee of intellectual truth, an authority of which the effect, when once its claims have by an initial act of private judgment been definitely acknowledged, shall be to exempt them from any further responsibility of a personal kind for the intellectual truth of the religious beliefs which they entertain" (*Essays Catholic and Critical*, p. 94).

THE MODERNIST MOVEMENT AND SCHOLARSHIP

For those of this cast of mind the decree *Pastor Aeternus* provided exactly what was required, but it raised serious difficulties at a time when new knowledge was pouring in from all directions and bringing with it changes in thought and outlook far vaster and more fundamental than those of the Reformation. The evidence that had been slowly accumulating since the days of Newton and Descartes reached its climax in

1860, since when the old barriers to free and unfettered inquiry have been breaking down everywhere. The results of scientific investigation cannot adequately be met by an obsolete obscurantism however ruthlessly it may be applied by an absolute authority. Herein lay the inherent weakness of Ultramontanism as it found expression in the Vatican decree of 1870 and in its more extreme exponents, such as Manning, who did not hesitate to affirm that "the appeal to antiquity is both a treason and a heresy. It is a treason because it rejects the Divine Voice of the Church at this hour, and a heresy because it denies that Voice to be Divine." But when that Voice solemnly declares, as in an encyclical at the time of the Malines Conversations in 1926, that "all who are truly Christ's believe, for example, the Conception of the Mother of God without stain of original sin with the same faith as they believe the mystery of the August Trinity, and the Incarnation of our Lord, just as they do the infallible teaching of the Roman Pontiff, according to the sense in which it has been defined by the Œcumenical Council of the Vatican," it is hardly likely to carry conviction to minds accustomed to think in relation to evidence based on sound foundations. Nor are the presuppositions those that are calculated to give a directive lead at a time of great intellectual unsettlement.

The foundation of the Catholic Institute in Paris in 1878 brought together a small group of scholars who, under the stimulating influence of Louis Duchesne and his pupil Alfred Loisy, claimed the right to apply modern scientific, historical and critical methods in their respective fields of inquiry. Here was an opportunity which might have become of immense service to the Church and the western world at a crucial moment if a policy of repression had not been adopted. Instead of directing the movement, Duchesne was suspended in 1885 for venturing to distinguish between fact and legend in ecclesiastical history, while in 1893 the less cautious Loisy was compelled to resign his Chair of Hebrew for using the established principles of critical interpretation in the study of the Scriptures. It is true that Loisy became fundamentally unorthodox and eventually reached a position which was quite irreconcilable with historic Christianity in any intelligible sense. But this hardly justifies the indiscriminate condemnation of the principles of Biblical criticism, in the encyclical *Providentissimus*, under the cover of the heretical conclusions of a particular scholar.

This unfortunate action opened the way for the setting up of the Biblical Commission in 1902 to act as a court of appeal in order to preserve the faithful from "erroneous" views and opinions from the side of scholarship. But its competence to form judgments on these matters may be gauged from the following affirmations: that no argument thus far adduced (i.e., in 1906) disproves the Mosaic authorship of the first five books of the Old Testament; that the creation stories in the book of Genesis represent "a narrative of events corresponding to objective reality and historical truth," including "the formation of the first woman from the first man"; that it is historically *certain* that St. John the son of Zebedee was the author of the Fourth Gospel; that the Epistle to the Hebrews is of "Pauline origin," and that the Gospels were written precisely in the order in which they appear in the New Testament to-day.

Faced with naïve obscurantism of these dimensions, which could be refuted by a boy or girl who had taken Divinity in the School Certificate Examination, it is not surprising that some Roman Catholic scholars like Loisy became in their turn "reactionary" in the direction of unorthodox liberalism, thereby bringing distrust of the Modernist movement as a whole, and giving some justification for its categorical condemnation by Pius X in his encyclical *Pascendi* on 8th September, 1907. This drastic action on the part of the Pope called forth a vigorous retort from George Tyrrell, an English Jesuit who had been expelled from the Society the previous year as a result of the private circulation of a provocative "Letter to a University Professor." The Holy See replied by excommunicating Tyrrell, and such was the reaction against the movement that even so orthodox and eminent a scholar as Baron von Hügel, whose learning, moderation and accuracy had won universal respect and recognition, lived in constant fear of ecclesiastical censure.

Nothing daunted, von Hügel always maintained that

Roman Catholicism could not permanently abide in a demonstrably vicious circle as to its fundamental logic. "In the long run," he said, "it will be found simply impossible to have one standard of historic method and proof for the reality of the Roman sojourn and martyrdom of St. Peter; and another, a conflicting standard of historical method and proof for the reality of the person of Moses, or the authenticity of the writings of Jeremiah and Ezekiel." And he adds, "a system cannot both claim to teach all the world and erect an impenetrable partition wall between itself and the educated portion of the world." Sooner or later it would seem the Ultramontane position will have to be modified. In the meantime the proscriptive decrees and encyclicals handicap Roman Catholic scholarship in making its proper contribution to present-day Biblical and theological thought and knowledge where historical and critical methods are involved which may lead to results at variance with the findings of the Biblical Commission.

SOCIAL PHILOSOPHY AND THE DOCTRINE OF THE STATE

In its attitude to social movements and the State a much more constructive policy is adopted, and as a result of recent encyclicals by Pius IX, Leo XIII and Pius XI, a Catholic philosophy of society is becoming established and consolidated. Capitalism, liberal democracy, socialism and communism have all been the subject of careful and critical investigation in relation to the Christian doctrine of man. In the words of Pius XI, "the State like the Church should form one body comprising many members, some excelling others in rank and importance, but all alike necessary to one another and solicitous for the common good." Man's rights, it is urged, depend not on his wealth but on his social function, and the State is a graduated hierarchy of "vocational groups which bind men together not according to the position they occupy in the labour market, but according to the diverse functions that they exercise in society."

Above the State is the spiritual authority which transcends the social, political and economic order, for, as Leo XIII submits, "the eternal law of God is the sole standard and rule of human liberty, not only in each individual man but also in the community." The principle of human freedom as understood in the English type of democracy is made subject to divine sovereignty inasmuch as "the true liberty of human society does not consist in every man doing what he pleases, for that would simply end in turmoil and confusion and bring on the overthrow of the State, but rather that through the injunctions of the civil law all may more easily conform to the prescriptions of the eternal law." As St. Thomas Aquinas recognized, the natural law by which men discern good and evil may be perverted or obscured by social causes, and, therefore, requires the restraining influence of a higher law transcending self-interest and self-preservation grounded in the eternal world.

The fundamental principle running through all the papal encyclicals on Catholic social philosophy since 1878, as Mr. C. Dawson has pointed out, is that of Christian civilization as "a concrete historical reality which derives its moral values and even its spiritual unity from its religious tradition. Europe is essentially a society of Christian peoples and nations—a society which derives its unity not from race or economic interest but from spiritual community, and that it is only by a restoration of this spiritual foundation that European order can be restored" (*The Judgement of the Nations*, p. 96). This conception of society in terms of a Corporative State and organic Spiritual Order was inherent in the medieval tradition of the Holy Roman Empire and the Augustinian ideal of the City of God with the Church as the dispensation of grace.

In a properly ordered world, according to St. Augustine, the Church and the secular Empire would be two aspects of the City of God, the one spiritual, the other temporal, organically united under one supreme heavenly rule, representing the continuation of the Incarnation transcending all the divisions, activities and limitations of human government, and consolidated in its one visible head, the Vicar and Viceroy of Christ.

Whether this be accepted or rejected as an ideal, the position and policy of the Holy See can only be rightly understood and appreciated in the light of these fundamental principles to which it has consistently held and still adheres. As Pius X declared, "it has always been the Church's motto to restore all things in Christ not only what directly depends on the divine mission of the Church to lead souls to God, but also, as we have explained, that which flows naturally from this divine mission, i.e., Christian civilization, in each and all of the elements that compose it."

BIBLIOGRAPHY

Amherst, J., *The History of the Catholic Emancipation and the Progress of the Catholic Church in Great Britain and Ireland.* 1886.

Adams, K., *The Spirit of Catholicism.* (E.T.) London, 1929.

Barrett, E. B., *The Jesuit Enigma.* London, 1928.

Bishop, E., *On the Origins of the Feast of the Conception of the Blessed Virgin Mary.* London, 1904.

Bury, J. B., *History of the Papacy in the Nineteenth Century.* London, 1930.

Creighton, M., *History of the Papacy.* Vol. V. London, 1919.

Dawson, C., *Judgement of the Nations.* London, 1943. *Religion and the Modern State.* London, 1938.

Jalland, T. G., *The Church and the Papacy.* London, 1944.

Kidd, B. J., *The Counter-Reformation.* London, 1933.

Lilley, A. L., Article "Modernism" in *Encyclopædia of Religion and Ethics* (Hastings). Vol. VIII (for bibliography).

Lilly, W. S., Article "England" in *Catholic Encyclopædia.* Vol. V. (for bibliography).

Longridge, W. H., *The Spiritual Exercises of St. Ignatius of Loyola.* London, 1919.

Nielsen, F., *History of the Papacy in the Nineteenth Century.* London, 1906.

Pollen, J. H., *St. Ignatius of Loyola.* Oxford, 1922. *English Catholics in the Reign of Elizabeth.* London, 1920.

Pullan, L., *Religion Since the Reformation.* Oxford, 1924.

Ranke, L. von., *History of the Popes.* Bohn, 1907.

Simpson, W. J. S., *French Catholics in the Nineteenth Century.* London, 1918.

Stebbing, G. A. *The Church in England.* London, 1921.

Thurston, H., Article "Jesuits" in *Encyclopædia of Religion and Ethics*. Vol. VII (for bibliography).

Vidler, A. R., *The Modernist Movement in the Roman Church*. Cambridge, 1934.

Ward, W., *Life of John Henry Cardinal Newman*. London, 1912. *Dawn of the Catholic Revival*. London, 1909. *Eve of Catholic Emancipation*. London, 1911.

CHAPTER VIII

ANGLICANISM

THE Evangelical Revival in England in the eighteenth century which reached its climax in the Methodist movement was not without its effects on the National Church and in saving the country from the apostasy of France in 1789. The literature and hymns of the period reveal the Evangelical fervour and zeal that were making their influence felt everywhere, and not least in Anglican circles. Thus, in Cambridge under the leadership of Charles Simeon (1759–1838), Fellow of King's, a group of earnest and serious-minded clergy and laity combined this type of piety and devotion with loyalty to the Establishment and the Book of Common Prayer, though they were more concerned with the salvation of individual souls than with the corporate life of the Church as a divinely-created visible Society. For them, like the continental Protestants and the English Non-conformists, the Church was primarily an invisible Communion in which all believers had their true and proper place and function, irrespective of ecclesiastical organization and allegiance, since it was the personal salvation of the individual that was the essence of all true Christianity. A passion for souls, in fact, was the dynamic of the movement, as in the Methodist Revival that preceded it. Therefore, it was marked by great pastoral activity and missionary enterprise which found expression in devoted work in the parishes and in the foundation of the Church Missionary Society in 1779 to evangelize Africa and the Far East.

THE ANGLICAN EVANGELICAL REVIVAL

As a product of the Romantic movement the Evangelical Revival in the Church of England was in reaction against rationalism and intellectualism, like its counterparts elsewhere, and emphasized the place of the emotions in religion, of human freedom and individualism. Interpreted in terms of theology, the Evangelical school centred its fervent preaching of the Gospel in a substitutionary doctrine of the Atonement coupled with that of justification by faith in the finished work of Christ. Starting from the Augustinian-Calvinistic assumption of the natural depravity of human nature, nothing less than a conscious experience of new birth resulting from the acceptance of salvation through the sacrifice of the Cross, could appease the wrath of God against sin and the sinner. The individual must make his own personal approach to the throne of grace without any instrumental or intermediary means, for Christ, and Christ alone, can save from eternal damnation. The sacraments were not repudiated, as by the Quakers, and within certain limits were held in esteem, but, since the "Spirit bloweth where it listeth," God is not tied to His own ordinances, and, therefore, in practice they tend to become subsidiary to the inward experience of salvation. Similarly, although redemption was regarded as a gift of grace and wholly independent of good works, this did not prevent pious Evangelicals from engaging actively in philanthropic enterprise. Thus, a series of notable social reforms, which included the amelioration of the hard lot of prisoners, the care of the destitute, the education of the poor and the abolition of the slave trade, was effected by men and women like William Wilberforce, Hannah More, Charles Kingsley and the "Clapham Sect," who were members of this school. Indeed, wherever their influence was felt the Evangelicals brought a truly Christian spirit to bear on their high endeavours.

Nevertheless, the fact remains that for them religion was something that stood apart from secular and everyday life. It was essentially an individual experience of the "elect" rather than the normal condition of a redeemed world manifesting itself in a philosophy embracing the whole of life. The weakness of Evangelicalism was the narrowness of its theology and general outlook. While isolated individuals developed a social and humanitarian conscience, the main concern of the movement as such was the salvation of souls. These "serious people," as they were called, "spoke to man's condition" as a sinner and sought to rescue individuals from spiritual ruin through a process of conversion. In culture, philosophy, science, literature and art, which constitute a considerable part of the human environment, they had little or no interest. Even their theology was confined to a naïve and crude soteriology, or doctrine of salvation, in which a penal interpretation was placed upon the sacrifice of Christ, difficult of either intellectual or ethical justification.

The Evangelical movement, therefore, made very little, if any, contribution to the thought and culture of the age, and while it awakened a new spiritual life in places like Cambridge, Clapham, Islington and Cheltenham, where it was strongly entrenched, it was not really an effective force in the Church of England, or the country at large, at the beginning of the nineteenth century. Thus, in 1822 there were only twelve Evangelical clergy in London, and in Oxford the school was confined almost exclusively to St. Edmund's Hall, one of the smallest and at that time least influential foundations. Its emotional appeal soon became a spent force and with the rise of the Calvinistic section of the party, its rigidity and Puritanism were in opposition to the prevailing Romanticism of the times. Devoid of an intellectual and cultural background, it was not easy to maintain indefinitely its former enthusiasm, and so by the end of the first quarter of the century its adherents were chiefly confined to a few fashionable watering-places and eclectic congregations in proprietary chapels elsewhere. Clearly if the National Church was to be resuscitated from its prolonged slumbers, the awakening must come from some other direction.

The new interest in the past created by the Romantic spirit was beginning to make itself felt in various directions. In Germany at Tübingen a radical school of Biblical criticism and historical research had arisen under the leadership of F. C. Bauer (1792–1860), in which the dialectical principles of the philosopher Hegel were applied to the study of the Scriptures with highly disturbing results from the point of view of orthodox Christianity. The "historical Jesus" became primarily a moral teacher rather than the saviour of mankind, who, under the influence of St. Paul and his followers, had been transformed into a legendary figure—"the Christ of the Creeds." The conflict between the "essential Christianity" of the original Jewish Christian community represented by St. Peter and the "Catholic theology" of St. Paul led in the Hegelian fashion to a synthesis at the end of the second century in the historic credal religion of Christendom. Albrecht Ritschl (1822–89) endeavoured to restore the position by asserting the authenticity of the New Testament in its witness to the Apostolic Church and its teaching, but he underestimated the literary and historical evidence upon which his Tübingen opponents rested their case.

In England Herbert Marsh, Regius Professor of Divinity at Cambridge, introduced this new German critical approach to Biblical studies, and the Dean of St. Paul's, H. H. Milman, adopted the same attitude to Jewish history. At Oxford the Senior Common Room at Oriel, as has been pointed out (cf. p. 145), contained some of the finest intellects in the university, and became the centre of a liberal movement. The group of intellectuals nicknamed "the Noetics" were composed of scholars of various traditions united in an endeavour to emancipate learning from hidebound authority and to promote freedom of thought and inquiry. They were not historians and had little acquaintance with the continental critical method, but in their outlook and presuppositions they were essentially progressive and in favour of reform in the teaching and practice of the Faith. The Provost of Oriel, Edward Hawkins, was a liberal High Churchman, like his predecessor Copleston. Whateley favoured disestablishment of the Church and Thomas Arnold, who became Headmaster of Rugby, foresaw the changes that were coming in the interpretation of the Bible and their effects on traditional theology. He was convinced, in fact, that nothing could save the Church of England, as it was then constituted, and proposed an undenominational union of all Christians other than Roman Catholics, Quakers and full-blown Unitarians.

THE OXFORD MOVEMENT

The Noetics, however, were only one section of the Oriel Common Room. In addition to them was another equally brilliant group who, while they were resolutely opposed to this political and theological liberalism, were also ardent reformers

L

and no less in despair of the Church. The rise to power of the Whigs and the passing of the Reform Bill in 1832, following immediately upon the repeal of the Test and Corporation Acts and the emancipation of Roman Catholics in 1829, constituted a challenge to the Establishment, which had been closely allied with the Tories. It only remained for ten bishoprics to be suppressed in Ireland to arouse John Keble to sound the alarm at the state of "national apostasy" in his Assize sermon in the University Church at Oxford on 14th July, 1933. This came as a call to action to the "Oriel Fellowship," who, in opposition to the Noetics, felt that the time had come for vigorous defence of the fundamental principles of Anglicanism.

Ten days later a small gathering was held at Hadleigh Rectory in Suffolk to consider a policy, and although Richard Hurrell Froude (who had just returned from a tour in the Mediterranean with John Henry Newman, then Vicar of the University Church) was the only Oriel man present, the conference represents the beginning of concerted action. Later in the year Newman began the publication of a series of provocative *Tracts for the Times* setting forth the teaching and practice of the Church as maintained by Hooker, the Caroline divines and the Non-jurors, in terms of a *via media*. An address to the Archbishop of Canterbury followed in 1834 in which 7,000 clergy and 230,000 heads of families professed adherence to the "apostolic doctrine and polity of the Church of England."

The inclusion of the Regius Professor of Hebrew, Edward Bouverie Pusey, among the authors of the tracts gave an academic distinction to the movement. As Newman said, he was "a host in himself; he was able to give a name, a form and a personality to what was without him a sort of mob." Moreover, he had first-hand knowledge of the new German critical methods in Biblical studies as well as being a learned Orientalist. On his return from Germany in 1827 he had published a defence of the Tübingen school though he soon retracted and became a relentless opponent of the critical investigation of the Scriptures and the champion of the Anglican orthodoxy in which he had been brought up from his youth. With this he combined an Evangelical tendency, derived perhaps from German

Pietism, which became more pronounced as the Tractarian movement developed, despite the strenuous opposition it encountered from the Evangelical school, as a reaction to "medievalism" and "superstition."

This was not a just or accurate estimate of the aim and outlook of the Tractarians, as the founders of the Oxford Movement were called. It is true, as we have seen (cf. p. 144), that a cleavage occurred in their ranks almost from the beginning which ultimately led to the secession to Rome of Newman, Ward (Fellow of Balliol), F. W. Faber (Fellow of University College), F. Oakeley (Fellow of Balliol) and J. B. Morris (Fellow of Exeter). But this minority was Ultramontane rather than medieval in its orientation, while the main body of the school had its roots deeply laid in the Laudian tradition. In so far as it went behind the Reformation, in accordance with the prevailing spirit of Romanticism the appeal was to antiquity and the authority of the Church of the Early Christian Fathers.

For them the Church of England was essentially the *via media* which through all its vicissitudes had preserved the Catholic episcopate, the creeds, the sacraments, and the faith of the undivided Church as set forth in Holy Writ and vindicated by the Œcumenical Councils. Coupled with this theological position went a passion for personal holiness and an intense moral discipline and religious earnestness comparable to that of the Evangelicals and the ethical integrity of the philosophy of Kant, which had permeated the Romantic Movement. Their devotion to the sacraments was prompted by their conviction that they were the divinely ordained means of grace for the development and deepening of the spiritual life of the faithful, for as Pusey stressed, "without holiness no man shall see the Lord." When the return to a Catholic way of life eventually found its natural expression in the restoration of the traditional modes of worship of "the whole and undivided Church," in accordance with the requirements of the Ornaments Rubric in the Book of Common Prayer, it was welcomed mainly because it was felt to be a fitting approach to the awful holiness and majesty of God. To ceremonial as such the early Tractarians attached little importance and made practically no changes in the customary order of public worship.

In the opinion of Pusey plain dresses were "more in keeping with the state of our Church, which is one of humiliation than the richer vestments used in Edward VI's reign." On the other hand they welcomed and encouraged the institution of retreats and the re-establishment of the religious life in the revival of the monastic orders, and advocated the celibacy of the clergy, because these restorations were felt to be important elements in the practice of the devout life.

The emphasis on an ascetic ideal of holiness and sanctification was in accord with the type of Anglican piety that had grown up in the days of Jeremy Taylor and William Law, and more recently under the influence of the Evangelical Revival and the Romantic Movement. The contribution of the Tractarians to the life and thought of the Church of England lay, therefore, in the recovery of the Laudian tradition on a clearly defined spiritual, ethical and theological basis. In this endeavour, however, they were handicapped by the fact that in practice the nation had so far departed from its Catholic and Caroline heritage that, as Newman discovered to his undoing, it was well nigh impossible to apply to the faith and practice of the Church of England at the beginning of the nineteenth century the standards maintained by "the whole and undivided Church" in the fifth century as an authoritative norm. So many new factors had emerged in the course of the intervening centuries in a divided Christendom which had witnessed a series of schisms and the growth of varying types of Christian experience and reactions to fresh situations, that to put the clock back to the opening centuries of the era was to attempt the impossible in the establishment of a systematic theology applicable to existing conditions. Thus, Newman was driven to repudiate the Tractarian conception of history in favour of "the development of Christian doctrine" in terms which anticipated the epoch-making treatise of Charles Darwin in 1859 in the biological sphere. In the second and later phases of the movement, the successors of these pioneers looked to the less remote medieval Church for their inspiration, while a minority endeavoured to re-interpret the Anglican tradition in terms of the faith and practice of the Counter Reformation as defined at the Council of Trent.

It was this last mentioned school (which had its roots in the Newman-Ward faction) that gave the Oxford Movement as a whole the appearance of being a subtle device to Romanize the Church of England; a belief that has never been completely obliterated from the popular mind, notwithstanding the tremendous influence the revival has had in changing the face of Anglicanism during the last century. To this movement must be attributed a new appreciation of the historical character and significance of the English Church and its essential Catholicity. This has found expression in the restoration of the decencies of worship, a more accurate interpretation of the rubrics of the Prayer Book, the restoration of a vigorous sacramental life, together with the establishment of religious houses (monasteries and nunneries) for men and women in ever increasing numbers, so that since the first profession made in St. Mary's, Oxford, in 1841 more Anglican communities have been set up in this country than existed at the time of the dissolution in 1536. In this matter at least Henry VIII has certainly been avenged by the Tractarians, and few would deny who are acquainted with their work in its manifold ramifications, that the restoration of the religious life in the Church of England has been one of the most beneficial results of the Movement to the Anglican Communion as a whole.

In the parishes, again, the zeal of pioneer priests who in the face of every kind of opposition devoted themselves unstinctedly to the service of God and the Church in the slums of great cities—is beyond all praise. Such men were Charles Lowder at St. Peter's, London Docks, G. R. Prynne at St. Peter's, Plymouth, A. H. Mackonochie and A. H. Stanton at St. Alban's, Holborn, the brothers Pollock at St. Alban's, Birmingham. As a recent writer has said, "the Anglo-Catholic might commit many kinds of mistake and folly. He might hold ludicrously inconsistent views about authority, and spend his leisure in baiting bishops, and hold services which had not even a bowing acquaintance with the Book of Common Prayer, but he worked. His hours were long, his endeavours were ceaseless, and he knew the technique of his job. He had a clear goal before him and he knew exactly how he meant to get there. In the vigour of his industry and in his life of constant sacrifice, no Protestant or Broad-Churchman could compare with him. If they had worked as he did, they and not the Anglo-Catholics would now be dominating the Church" (R. Lloyd, *The Church of England in the Twentieth Century* (1946) p. 136). It was the same spirit they revealed in missionary enterprise as is shown, for example, in the noble record of the Universities Mission to Central Africa and the Oxford Mission to Calcutta, with their long lines of heroes, and saints.

Where the movement failed, especially in its early stages, was in its insularity and isolation from the scientific and theological thought of the age. If, as was maintained, the Church of England was one "branch" of the undivided Church, it was manifestly only one part of the whole, with its own peculiarities and independent history. To argue from the particular to the general is to court disaster. Anglicanism is an attempt, not wholly unsuccessful, to retain and maintain in one all-embracing communion the proved spiritual value both of the sacramental system and the authoritative teaching of the historic faith of Christendom, with a sufficiently large measure of freedom to make possible the assimilation of new knowledge and truth as and when it becomes known. This satisfies the conditions of a *via media*, but it is not so easily reconciled with those of an undivided Christendom before the body corporate had been rent asunder by ecclesiastical and denominational cleavages and new knowledge had poured in to wreak havoc among all the established positions of thought and practice.

ANGLICAN ISOLATION

Cut off from official intercourse with contemporary theological movements on the Continent first by the breach with Rome in 1534 and later by that with Geneva in 1660, the Church of England had been thrown back on its own resources ever since the Restoration, and in consequence its spiritual horizon was limited and insular. Rationalism, German pietism and Romanticism, it is true, had repercussions respectively on English Deism, Methodism and the Evangelical and Tractarian

Revivals, but in its official aspect, the Establishment looked with disfavour on all innovations and foreign influences. Even the universities, where most of the clergy were trained, were its own preserves and, therefore, on the theological side they lacked the breadth of vision and the cross-fertilization of scholarship wider contacts would have provided. Thus, it must be admitted that in the first half of the last century the Church of England was ill-prepared and ill-equipped to meet the tremendous onslaught of new knowledge that was rushing towards it with all the force of an avalanche.

The Evangelicals were completely out of touch with the realities of the situation and could only meet the attacks of critical scholars, rationalists and free thinkers by the assertion of the infallibility of Scripture, regardless of the fact that this was the very doctrine that was being challenged on all hands by a forbidding and accumulating weight of evidence. The Tractarians were too absorbed in vindicating the Catholic heritage and moralism of their particular conception of the *via media* in all its Patristic splendour to be concerned with the trend of thought in the great world outside their own relatively narrow circle of ecclesiastical controversy, earnest moral endeavour and zealous parochial activity. Newman, it is true, felt his way towards a theory of development in Christian doctrine which placed him among the harbingers of the intellectual revolution of 1860, but which led him outside the Anglican Communion altogether. And his departure bereft the Oxford Movement of one of its most creative thinkers, and left it more static and "pre-evolutionary" than ever, confirmed in its obscurantism and insularity.

The Darwinian Revolution

It should be remembered, however, that the National Church and its teachers, be they Catholic, Evangelical or Erastian, were strictly in accord with the prevailing thought of their age in maintaining what seems to us to be an obscurantist position, viewing the situation in the light of present-day knowledge. A century ago thought moved on a very different plane. Then the commonplaces of to-day in the matter of the scientific interpretation of the universe and its processes, and the critical study of the Bible, were confined to a very small and "advanced" group of thinkers. Thus, for example, the idea of the fixity of species had been steadfastly maintained by the leading botanist of the eighteenth century (i.e., Linnæus, 1707-76), and in the next century this view was confirmed by the most distinguished French anatomist, Cuvier, while the most violent and uncompromising opponents of the Darwinian hypothesis, when it was first enunciated, was Richard Owen, Regius Professor of Anatomy at Oxford, and Adam Sedgwick, one of the foremost geologists of the time. As Darwin's magnanimous colleague, A. R. Wallace, affirmed, "the great majority of naturalists, and almost without exception the whole literary and scientific world held firmly to the belief that species were realities, and had not been derived from other species by any process accessible to us—but by some totally unknown process removed so far from ordinary reproduction that it was usually spoken of as 'special creation'" (*Darwinianism* (1889) p. 8). While in *The Origin of Species*, Darwin himself declared that "all our greatest geologists unanimously, often vehemently, maintained the immutability of species" (Inst. Ed., p. 310).

Therefore, in opposing the evolutionary hypothesis when it was first set forth in the middle of the last century, theologians can hardly be accused of mere "reactionary" motives, however much they may have had their own reasons for joining in the almost universal condemnation. They were merely following where the expert led the way, and in fairness to authoritative scientific opinion it must be remembered that the evidence available in 1859, though on the whole calculated to make a strong case in favour of the conjecture so persuasively argued in *The Origin of Species*, was very far from having been definitely established. It was most unfortunate, nevertheless, that the Bishop of Oxford, Samuel Wilberforce, intervened in the controversy at the meeting of the British Association in his cathedral city in 1860, as he was quite incompetent to pass an opinion on an issue of such complexity, and his action gave the anti-clericals an opportunity to brand the Church as obscurantist. But it now seems that actually he was the mouthpiece of Richard Owen, and, therefore, really voicing the opinion of the scientific opposition rather than expressing that of the Church.

Samuel Wilberforce had been brought up in an Evangelical home and at Oxford he read the Honours School of Mathematics (in which incidentally he was placed in the first class), so that he had had neither a biological nor a theological training. On proceeding to ordination he became the most prominent member of the High Church party, as distinct from Anglo-Catholic Tractarianism, from which he stood as much aloof as from the Evangelicalism of his youth. He was equally opposed to the liberalism of the Broad Church party. The "Central Churchmanship" which at that time the former "High Churchmen" represented, was then full of vigour, and no one was more indefatigable than Wilberforce in stimulating the new zeal for parochial work and priestly efficiency that was becoming a feature of this school. To the training of ordination candidates he paid particular attention and the theological college at Cuddesdon set a standard through his influence which has become a norm in the Church of England. Again, it was he who was largely responsible for the revival of Convocation as the regenerating centre of Church life from which a new ecclesiastical organization was to proceed.

Cumbered about much serving, however, he was less alive to the significance of the new movements of thought that were taking shape in the intellectual world around him. He threw his weight against the appointment to the See of Hereford of R. D. Hampden, the Regius Professor of Divinity at Oxford, whose Bampton Lectures in 1832 on *The Scholastic Philosophy in Relation to Christian Theology* seemed to cast doubt upon the doctrines of the Trinity and the Atonement. Here he had legitimate grounds for his strictures, but when he took up the cudgels against the new biology, not only was he fighting for a lost cause but he was entering the lists without any adequate weapons of defence. In pouring scorn and ridicule on a hypothesis he was incapable of understanding, or of weighing the evidence on which it was based, he began a controversy between science and religion at the most inopportune moment, which has done incalculable disservice to

M

the cause he championed. It is, however, to the credit of Canon Tristram that he was the first zoologist publicly to accept the theory of natural selection, while Charles Kingsley was an equally steadfast supporter of the evolutionists, despite the unfortunate lead given to the Church by Wilberforce. Their courageous intervention mitigated the mischief done by the impetuous Bishop of Oxford, and even so jaundiced an anti-clerical as T. H. Huxley was forced to admit his surprise at the broadmindedness shown by the "black coats and white cravats" to "the horrible paradoxes of 1860," soon destined to become "the commonplaces of schoolboys" and facts which "no rational man could dispute."

ANGLICAN LIBERALISM

Before the publication of *The Origin of Species*, Anglican scholars, however, were beginning to feel their way towards a new apologetic. The Oriel Noetics, as we have seen, had broken away from the old tradition, and their work was carried on by such thinkers as F. W. Robertson, of Brighton, A. P. Stanley, subsequently Dean of Westminster, and F. W. Farrar who became Dean of Canterbury, with the influential support of Lord Tennyson. The year after the appearance of Darwin's great book a volume of *Essays and Reviews* was produced to "encourage free and honest discussion of Biblical topics." The Bible, it was maintained by Jowitt, Master of Balliol, in his contribution, should be interpreted like any other book, and the Savilian Professor of Astronomy at Oxford, Baden Powell, defended the Darwinian theory. Before the flood of criticism occasioned by the volume had subsided, Bishop Colenso, of Natal, in highly provocative language, subjected the Pentateuch to a critical examination and decided against its Mosaic authorship and the historicity of the opening chapters of Genesis. This raised a further storm in which Pusey and the Evangelical Lord Shaftesbury joined forces, and with the general approval of the clergy and laity, the author was excommunicated by the Metropolitan of Cape Town. This led to a schism in the South African Church which lasted until 1891.

In the meantime, however, wiser counsels were beginning to

prevail. In 1870 the Convocation of Canterbury urged the need of a revised version of the Bible and four months later a distinguished company of linguistic scholars, which included representatives of several other denominations, once again assembled in the Jerusalem chamber in Westminster Abbey to begin the gigantic task which resulted in the production of a new and more accurate translation of the New Testament in 1881 and of the Old Testament in 1885, to which the Apocrypha was added in 1896. At Cambridge Westcott, Hort and Lightfoot had been working on the original text of the New Testament for some time, while at Oxford S. R. Driver, the successor of Pusey, was engaged in similar studies on the Old Testament, paying particular attention to critical problems. In Scotland a presbyterian divine, William Robertson Smith, had broken new ground in the investigation of the origins of the religion of the Semites in the light of recent anthropological research. This cost him his Chair at the Free Church College, Aberdeen, but his subsequent appointment to the Professorship of Arabic at Cambridge provided him with an official status and excellent opportunities for carrying on his pioneer work. In this task he found a ready ally in his friend, J. G. Frazer, who was then beginning his vast collection of data that eventually went to the making of *The Golden Bough*, the first edition of which appeared in 1890, as a prelude to the twelve volumes into which it grew between 1911 and 1915.

As knowledge increased and the new methods of Biblical study became better understood, the new learning permeated the Church of England as a whole. At Oxford Charles Gore, as Principal of Pusey House (an Anglo-Catholic centre in the university established to perpetuate the memory of the Tractarian leader whose name it bore) gathered round him a group of scholars between 1875 and 1885 who "felt compelled for their own sake (as university teachers) no less than that of others, to attempt to put the Catholic faith into its right relation to modern intellectual and moral problems." The result was a volume of essays entitled *Lux Mundi*, in which the cardinal doctrines of the Church and the Sacraments, for which the Tractarians had contended, were interpreted in terms applicable to the thought of the age. Of course to the rigid orthodoxy of the founders of the Oxford Movement the liberalism of *Lux Mundi* would have been anathema, and when the volume appeared it had a hostile reception from their successors, led by Canon Liddon of St. Paul's. Nevertheless, it virtually laid the foundations of an apologetic which has become generally adopted in the universities and by intelligent people throughout the Anglican Communion. Thus, in the present century when a similar band of scholars were drawn together by "a common desire to attempt a fresh exposition and defence of the Catholic faith" in the belief that "Catholic unity and authority and the critical movement" can be and must be brought into synthesis, the new volume, entitled *Essays Catholic and Critical*, under the editorship of the Dean of Winchester (Dr. E. G. Selwyn), the *Lux Mundi* position could be taken for granted. Similarly, the Evangelicals have now adopted a liberal "group movement" which aims at maintaining the zeal and piety of their forebears with an enlightened attitude towards present-day intellectual problems and current knowledge in such matters as Biblical criticism (cf. T. Guy Rogers, *Liberal Evangelicalism*, 1923). Outside these two fundamentally orthodox schools of thought a more radical Modernism finds expression in "The Modern Churchman's Union" led by Dr. Major and a group of distinguished scholars, who feel, for the most part, that nothing less than a drastic restatement of the credal basis of historical Christianity is required to meet the intellectual situation.

Thus, the insularity, Erastianism, intransigence and obscurantism of post-Restoration Anglicanism have now been abandoned, except for a few vociferous but uninfluential diehards who are still thinking in terms of bygone ages. The "Broad Churchmanship" of the last century, however, can hardly be said to hold the field. The general outlook has changed so fundamentally since it took its stand for unfettered critical inquiry, and while the principles for which it contended are now not only conceded but widely established, the ideals of the Librral Protestanism as expressed, for example, by Adolf von Harnack in terms of social reform, ethical teaching, political liberalism, progressive organization and immanental theology, are certainly not in the ascendant. These belonged essentially to the age of phenomenal prosperity in which they arose when "modern man was up and doing" everywhere, and not least in the feverish activity that characterized the Church of England at the turn of the century.[1]

The fateful year 1914 marks the great divide, but it is probably true to say that the translation in 1910 of a book by Albert Schweitzer under the title of *The Quest of the Historical Jesus*, called a halt to the progressive march of the Harnack type of liberalism in the Anglican Communion. Not only did Schweitzer dispose of the "Jesus of history" as a social reformer and teacher of ethics, but he substituted for the earlier Modernist interpretation of Christ an apocalyptic theory. For him Our Lord was the forerunner of the Messiah Who endeavoured to force God to set up His Kingdom in a catastrophic divine intervention but died on the Cross disillusioned and defeated. "The Son of Man was buried in the ruins of the falling eschatological world; there remained alive only Jesus 'the Man'."

This revolutionary and disconcerting interpretation of the Gospel occupied the attention of the Church Congress which met at Cambridge the same year (1910), and there could be little doubt that Schweitzer had undermined the German Modernist position which had not been without its influence on English Liberal theologians. At least he and his followers had shown that the coming of the Kingdom of God with power and in judgment was the dominant theme of the Gospels, however unacceptable and untenable might be the eschatological solution of the problem he offered. It only required such a catastrophic event as that which burst on the world on the 4th August four years later to destroy once and for all the idea of progressive civilization moving to its Utopian goal in an orderly sequence under the guidance of science and the humanitarian and ethical teaching of the "Jesus of history." The complacent optimism of immanentism and absolute idealism gave place to a transcendental theology of "crisis" and a new type of apologetic in which the real historical problem

[1] This was the period of intense organization in great parishes like Leeds and St. Mary's, Portsea, of public school missions and slum settlements, such as Oxford House at Bethnal Green and Cambridge House at Camberwell.

was not so much the question of the authorship and date of the several documents of the New Testament, but whether or not the Gospels give a true representation of the conception of Jesus as the redemptive Messiah. The interest shifted from the relations of science and religion, the problems of Biblical criticism and of the origins of Christianity —matters upon which the Modernists had been concentrating their attention for a quarter of a century—to the revelation of God in the significant events of history.

This new emphasis on divine transcendence reached its height in continental Protestantism in the theology of Karl Barth and Emil Brunner. God, it was claimed, is not primarily the object of human knowledge. He is the living, active Spirit, choosing, laying hold of and possessing man, coming to him from without—i.e., from beyond knowledge and from beyond history—and speaking to him in an oracular "Word of God" from His sublime and solitary heights in eternity, interpreted by the inner witness of the Holy Spirit. It was virtually the old cry of the Reformers; "Not by works, but by faith: man is nought, God's glory is all," and the repudiation of a Christian philosophy or a Christian civilization. Such a baseless dogmatism, of course, was merely a reaction against the complacent immanence and subjectivism of nineteenth-century Modernism and Pragmatism. But inasmuch as it corrected in an extreme form an equally radical intellectual liberalism, probably it served its purpose in Central Europe at a time of urgent "crisis," when sound judgment is hardly to be expected.

In England not only was the situation less drastic in 1919, but the way already had been prepared for a more even redress of the balance by Anglican thinkers such as J. R. Illingworth, a member of the *Lux Mundi* group, and from the Roman Catholic side, by Baron von Hügel. God, it had been argued, cannot be immanent in a creation that He does not transcend nor transcendent over a world unless He is immanent within it. The two aspects of divine activity must be brought into a living relationship with our own experience wherein spirit moves in a realm above bodily organism, and yet is in the organism animating it (cf. Illingworth, *Divine Immanence*,

1898, and *Divine Transcendence*, 1911). Philosophers like W. R. Sorley and C. C. J. Webb were beginning to stress divine personal sovereignty standing over against the created universe, and von Hügel maintained that while in any full-blooded religion there must be an element of the "given" to admit "the fresh air of heaven," proper attention must also be paid to the historical and rational elements as well as to the emotional and mystical aspects of spiritual experience.

Until the critical method had sorted out the documents and drawn a distinction between fact and legend, the transitory and the permanent in the Biblical revelation, little headway could be made in a sound apologetic calculated to carry conviction to thinking minds in a post-war world when the first shock of "crisis" had passed. As E. C. Hoskyns and F. N. Davey pointed out in a pioneer work in this movement, aimed at the recovery of a Biblical theology, "the riddle of the New Testament is a theological riddle which is insoluble apart from the solution of an historical problem." The importance of what may be called the "critical period" at the turn of the century should not be minimized because its work was essential as a preliminary stage leading up to the more constructive phase of interpretation. Liberal Protestantism failed because it left unanswered the crucial questions, what was the relation between Jesus of Nazareth and the primitive Church? What lies behind the theology of St. Paul and the Johannine literature? A new school of "Form-criticism," therefore, had to arise to try to interpret the Christ of faith whom the Gospels describe, which is as near as we can get to the "Jesus of history."

Moreover, the modern world in the middle of the twentieth century, amid all the stress and strain of tumultuous happenings, is seeking a "Word of God" as an interpretation of the actual situation. To-day it is the social, ethical and political bearings of Christianity that are uppermost in the thought of the age rather than the intellectual problems that dominated the scene in the prosperous and progressive period of advance and security. A "Word of God" is needed for a "Day of God," as Barth and his inspirer, Kierkegaard, the Danish philosopher before him, realized. This presupposes a conception of transcendence and revelation; "the cutting across of purposes by events," as Professor C. H. Dodd would say; of God speaking from beyond this world rather than in the processes of nature and the harmonious reign of inviolable law and order; and acting in history both as judgment and as power of renewal, demanding a response from man.

As this is the conception of revelation which finds abundant illustration in Holy Scripture, alike in the Old and New Testaments, it is not surprising that the present tendency among theologians is a return to Biblical theology with special emphasis on the interpretation of significant historical events rather than on the analysis and dating of documents. "From faith to faith" has become perhaps a somewhat overworked dictum in recent years, and with the temporary eclipse of liberalism everywhere in Church and State (despite a great deal of talk about "freedom"), a "flight from reason" is manifest on all sides. In reaction against the former critical methods, the Bible is being expounded mystically by the Bible, often with almost complete disregard of scientific and historical exegesis. The incarnational theology of Westcott and the *Lux Mundi* school, with its idealistic philosophic background, is now giving place to a theology of redemption as more in keeping with the present shattered state of the world and the Neo-Calvinistic dogmatism of Barthianism. The absence of a satisfactory Anglican philosophy, and the need of some basis of faith in reason, has produced a revival of scholasticism in a Neo-Thomist movement in line with that which has considerable vogue in continental Roman Catholicism, which is now gaining ground among the younger Anglican scholars at Oxford and elsewhere.

With all traditions, ideologies and theologies in a state of disintegration it is impossible to predict with any degree of precision the shape of things to come. So far as Anglicanism is concerned, the three schools that have dominated the Communion during the last century give every appearance of having played their parts, at any rate for the time being, and while each has made a permanent contribution to the Church it has served with zeal and devotion, the future does not seem very likely to lie with any one to the exclusion of the others.

Indeed, Evangelicalism, Anglo-Catholicism and Modernism at the moment are equally spent forces as the spear-heads of a religious revival in this country. Whether the present evangelistic efforts will meet with more success than the ill-fated "National Mission of Repentance and Hope" in 1916, time will prove, but it cannot be denied that in the interval between the two great wars the Church of England has made a gallant attempt to set its house in order, if the results still leave much to be done.

The passing of the Enabling Act in 1919 has made possible many long overdue administrative reforms, from the division of unwieldly dioceses to the inauguration of a pension scheme for the clergy and the disposal of unworkable parsonage houses.[1] The financial situation, however, is precarious, existing resources being only sufficient to provide hardly tolerable salaries for two-thirds of the parochial clergy, while loss of income from royalties and investments, coinciding with a phenomenal rise in the cost of living and a fall of purchasing power, has created a precarious position at a time when an unparalleled demand is being made for new parishes and churches in the rapidly multiplying housing estates on the outskirts of great cities. The training of impecunious ordination candidates, hitherto left mainly to such enterprising institutions as the Community of the Resurrection at Mirfield, with its university hostel at Leeds, and the Society of the Sacred Mission with its seminary at Kelham, and the generosity of private sponsors, has now become the responsibility of the Church as a whole. But heavy as is the drain on the resources of a greatly impoverished exchequer, that an heroic attempt is being made to implement these and many similar schemes, shows that the Anglican Communion is alive to the needs of the age.

As Randall Davidson declared at the end of his great episcopate in his farewell sermon at Canterbury on 4th November, 1928 (immediately after the parliamentary debacle

[1]The rejection by Parliament of the proposed revision of the Prayer Book in 1927-28, adopted and sanctioned by Convocation and the other official assemblies of the Church, was an anomaly which reveals that notwithstanding the Enabling Act, the State connection can still be a serious handicap when a persistent minority can override decisions of properly constituted ecclesiastical authority.

over the revision of the Prayer Book), "looking back over fifty years of serious service," it was his firm conviction that "the Church of England to-day whatever her difficulties, is far stronger, far more zealous, has a truer vision of God's purpose, and is more united—yes, more united in effort and in prayer—than it was when my working years began." And to him and his leadership this achievement in no small measure was due. Cathedrals have become dynamic centres of the spiritual life of the dioceses, parish churches in great cities are the scenes of ceaseless activity, and the countryside owes more to the Church and its school and rectory than it had realized until these consolidating and edifying influences have been removed by the amalgamation of benefices in rural areas. Such widespread and influential organizations as the Mothers' Union, the Girls' Friendly Society and the Church of England Men's Society have borne witness to the vitality of the Church in the twentieth century, while in ministering to all sorts and conditions of men, from tramps and prisoners to organized labour and students, the Church Army, the Industrial Christian Fellowship and the Student Christian Movement (an interdenominational society in which the Church plays an important part) are among many institutions engaged in aggressive evangelism and the propagation of the Faith. The same is true of its missionary enterprise in all parts of the world.

Anglicanism is a unique phenomenon which has grown out of the English constitution and the peculiar history of the nation and empire. As a living organism it has followed its own course and determined its own destiny, refusing to be prescribed within the limits set for it by any of the traditions and movements it has comprehended, or which has sought to capture it. Grounded and rooted in Western Christendom it grew to maturity, and largely under the influence of the Reformation, blossomed forth as an independent growth. After a period of quiescence it had to render its own life and truth explicit in the invigorating atmosphere of modern thought and knowledge in an industrialized age in which Great Britain led the way. As in the Reformation period it occupied an intermediate position between Rome and Geneva, so to-day, when new reactions to a disorganized world are cutting across the former party allegiances, its role seems to be to stand between Neo-Calvinist obscurantism, Ultramontane dogmatism and Marxist materialism, on its own historic basis of Scripture, tradition and reason. The wheel having gone nearly full circle, it is not improbable that it may come to rest more or less where Anglicanism first became aware of its independent individuality, neither Roman nor Calvinist but at once Catholic and Reformed, with a positive doctrine and discipline of its own.

To return unreservedly to Hooker and the Caroline Divines, who laid the foundations of the tradition, of course would be disastrous, twentieth-century conditions being so vastly different from those of the seventeenth century. To be effective a religion always must exercise its functions in relation to the complex of contemporary culture and civilization, and the existing structure and ethos of the society in which it occurs. The principles, however, for which these pioneers contended were fundamentally sound, essentially English and eminently practical. Indeed, the history of the Church in England reveals that what they strove to accomplish must be preserved if stability is to be maintained. While doubtless in the future, as has been the case in the past, particular emphasis will be given by different schools of thought to their respective theologies, the English Church, as a composite whole, like the nation of which historically it is an integral part, fulfils its proper purpose as a consolidating force when it is true to itself and its own traditions evolved out of its peculiar historical circumstances, geographical environment and inherent genius.

BIBLIOGRAPHY

Bell, G. K. A., *Randall Davidson*. Oxford, 2nd Ed. 1938.

Brilioth, Y. T., *The Anglican Revival*. London, 1925.

Carpenter, S. C., *The Church and the People*, 1789–1889. London, 1933.

Church, R., *The Oxford Movement*. London, 1891.

Garbett, C., *The Church of England*. London, 1947.

Gore, C., *Lux Mundi*. London, 1889.

Henson, Hensley, H., *Retrospect of an Unimportant Life*. Oxford, 1942–1943.

Hoskyns, E. C., Davey, F. N., *The Riddle of the New Testament*. London, 1931.

Lloyd, R., *The Church of England in the Twentieth Century*. London, 1946.

Major, H. D. A., *English Modernism*. London, 1927.

Ollard, S. L., *A Short History of the Oxford Movement*. London, 1915.

Patterson, M. W., *A History of the Church of England*. London, 1909.

Prestige, G. L., *Charles Gore*. London, 1935.

Rogers, T. G., *Liberal Evangelicalism*. Vol. I. London, 1923. *The Inner Light*. Vol. II. London, 1925.

Russell, G. W. E., *A Short History of the Evangelical Movement*. London, 1915.

Selwyn, G. C., *Essays Catholic and Critical*. London, 1926. *The Approach to Christianity*. London, 1925.

Smyth, C., *Simeon and Church Order*. Cambridge, 1940.

Stewart, H. C., *A Century of Anglo-Catholicism*. London, 1929.

Storr, V. F., *Freedom and Liberty. A Study of Liberal Evangelicalism*. London, 1940. *The Development of English Theology in the Nineteenth Century*, 1800–60. London, 1913.

Tulloch, J., *Movements of Religious Thought in Britain*. London, 1885.

Wand, J. W. C., *The Anglican Communion*. Oxford, 1948.

Webb, C. C. J., *Religious Thought in the Oxford Movement*. London, 1928. *A Century of Anglican Theology*. Oxford, 1923. *A Study of Religious Thought in England Since* 1850. London, 1933.

INDEX

A

Acton, Lord, 143
Aidan, St., 23
Alban, St., 16
Alcuin, 33, 34f
Alfred the Great, 36
Amesbury, 15f
Anabaptists, 73, 97, 117
Anglican Church, the, 90, 103, 107, 110, 158ff, 177
Anglo-Catholic movement, the, 165 (see Tractarians)
Anglo-Saxon Christianity, 28
——invasion, 18f
——missionary enterprise, 32ff
——schools, 32ff
Andrewes, Lancelot, 90, 92, 95
Anselm, 44f, 62
Aquinas, St. Thomas, 62, 147, 155
Arthur, King, legend of, 13
Aragon, Catherine of, 69, 78
Arminianism, 93, 117, 125
Articles, the Six, 73, 77
——the Ten, 72
——the Thirty-nine, 83
Augustine, St. of Canterbury, 17, 21, 23ff
——of Hippo, 62, 147, 155, 159
Avalon, isle of, 13

B

Baptists, 97, 113, 116ff
Barth, K., 174f
Bauer, F. C., 160
Beaker folk, 11, 15, 26, 28, 81
Becket, Thomas, 49ff
Bede, the Venerable, 16, 33ff
Benedict, St., 38
Benefices, farming of, 52
——incomes of, 53
Biblical Commission, the, 153

Biscop, Benedict, 33, 37
Boniface, 35
Book of Common Prayer, the, 1549, 75f, 83
——1552, 78, 83
——1662, 100
——1928, 177
Booth, William, 127
Britain, origin of civilization in, 11ff
——pre-Roman, 11ff, 15
Browne, Robert, 113f
Brünner, E., 174
Butler, Joseph, 106

C

Calvinism, 74, 76, 93, 104, 113ff, 160
Candida casa at Whithorn, 17
Cathedrals, 58, 71
Celibacy of the clergy, 37, 58
Celtic Christianity, 17ff, 24ff
——its monastic organization, 19ff, 26
Challoner, Richard, 141
Charles I, 96f
——II, 98, 113
Church Army, the, 178
Church Missionary Society, 158
Church, the, beginnings of, in Britain, 16ff
Clapham sect, the, 159
Clarendon, Constitutions of, 50
Clarke, W. K. L., 107
Colenso, Bishop, 170
Collegiate churches, 58
Colman, 25
Columbia, St., 22, 24
Congregationalism, 133ff (see Independents)
Continental influence in Britain, 11ff 19, 23ff, 28
Cranmer, Thomas, 69f, 73, 79f
Cromwell, Oliver, 96f, 113

181